Dislecksia: The Book
Companion to the Documentary Film

By

Harvey Hubbell V

Edited by Julie Costanzo and Phyllis C. Orlowski

2012

Who are They?

1 – **1950's Teacher** (USA)

2 – **Harvey Hubbell V**
Director, Producer
Dislecksia: The Movie

3 – **Harvey Hubbell V**
Third Grade

4 – **Stephen J. Cannell**
Writer, Producer

5 – **Billy Bob Thornton**
Musician, Actor,
Filmmaker

6 – **Thomas Edison**
Inventor

7 – **Eric Gardner**
Producer, Editor,
Dislecksia: The Movie

8 – **Dr. Samuel Orton**
Physician

9 – **Joe Pantoliano**
Actor, Producer, Director

10 – **Harvey Hubbell V**
Twelfth Grade

11 – **Harvey Hubbell V**
First Grade

12 – **Sarah Joy Brown**
Actress

13 – **Harvey Hubbell V**
(2005)

14 – **Albert Einstein**
Theoretical Physicist

15 – **Guinevere Eden**
Past President, IDA

16 – **Billy Blanks**
Inventor of Tae Bo

17 – **Dee Rosenberg**
Director of Education,
Newgrange School

18 – **Kendrick Meek**
U.S. Representative of Florida's
17th district

19 – **Olivia Hanson**
Student, Forman School

20 – **Wendy Welshans**
Teacher, Forman School

21 – **Tom West**
Author

22 – **Keaghan Hamilton**
Student, Forman School

23 – **Sylvia Richardson**
Past President, Orton Dyslexia
Society

24 – **R. Christopher Blake**
Entertainment Attorney

25 – **Roger Saunders**
Past President, Orton Dyslexia
Society

26 – **Milos Forman**
Director, Writer, Actor

27 – **Ken Pugh**
President, Haskins Laboratories

28 – **Aimee Santos**
Co-Producer, *Dislecksia: The Movie*

29 – **Mark Seidenberg**
Professor, University of Wisconsin

30 – **Jeffrey Gilger**
Associate Dean, Purdue University

31 – **Gordon Sherman**
Executive Director, Newgrange
School

32 – **Nancy Hislop**
Harvey's sister

33 – **Linda Peterson**
Harvey's sister

34 – **Anna Gillingham**
Educator, Psychologist

35 – **Jeanne Simpson**
Harvey's mom

36 – **Jack Horner**
Paleontologist, Author

37 – **Barbara Corcoran**
Founder,
Corcoran Group

38 – **Diana King**
Founder, Kildonan School

39 – **Margie Gillis**
Director, Haskins Literacy
Initiative

40 – **Arlene Sonday**
Founder, Sonday Systems

41 – **Evelyn Russo**
Mentor, Haskins Literacy
Initiative

42 – **Winston Churchill**
Prime Minister,
United Kingdom

43 – **David Boies**
Attorney

44 – **Voncille Wright**
Jo'Von's mom

45 – **Harvey Hubbell IV**
Harvey's dad

46 – **Delos Smith**
Economist

47 – **Jo'Von Wright**
Student, Forman School

48 – **Gayle Cole**
Harvey's sister

49 – **Gamera**
Japanese Giant Monster

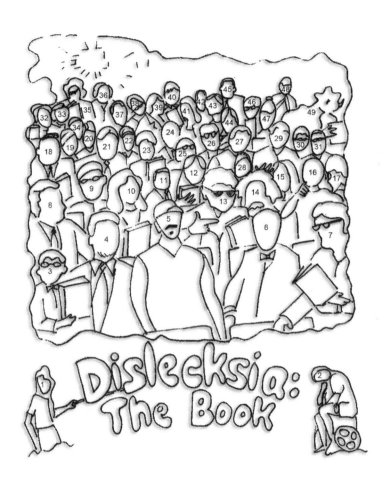

ISBN: 146377995X

ISBN 13: 9781463779955

Library of Congress Control Number: 2011914676

CreateSpace Independent Publishing Platform

North Charleston, South Carolina

Dedicated to
Steve J. Link,
my high school guidance counselor, advocate, and friend

How To Use This Book

Dyslexia is a complicated subject, a learning difference that affects everyone in a unique way. What follows in these chapters are hypotheses about dyslexia from brain scientists and life experiences from dyslexics and their families. Some of these stories may seem conflicting, but all lead back to the fact that no two dyslexics are the same. This book was not created as a thorough study on dyslexia, but as a way to provide beneficial information that could not fit into our documentary.

This book is broken down into eleven chapters. Each of the chapters starts off with a question: The first question is *What is Dyslexia?* Harvey Hubbell V, director and producer of *Dislecksia: The Movie* gives his response to the question first, then brain specialists, the dyslexics, the educators, and other advocates give their responses. At the back of the book, you'll find an alphabetical list of these people (the contributors) and a brief bio of each person.

Dislecksia: The Book, Companion to the Documentary Film features thirty-five student profiles that include a photo, along with the school they attend and a brief statement from or about them. These students represent those that have chosen to leave their public schools to find a more appropriate education for themselves. Following the contributors, you will find a listing of each student and their school.

Throughout the book you will also find sketches done by elementary school age children from Newgrange School in Hamilton, New Jersey and Greater Plains Elementary School in Oneonta, New York. We asked the children to sketch what it feels like to "get it," or understand what the teacher was teaching, and what it feels like to "not get it." The names of the student artists can be found at the back of the book.

Dislecksia: The Book, Companion to the Documentary Film can be used in a variety of ways, whether you've seen *Dislecksia: The Movie* or not. Feel free to skip back and forth between chapters, simply omit chapters that might not be of interest to you, or read the entire book from cover to cover. This book was designed for dyslexics, advocates, legislators, researchers, parents, educators, and newcomers to the world of dyslexia.

Dislecksia: The Book
Table of Contents

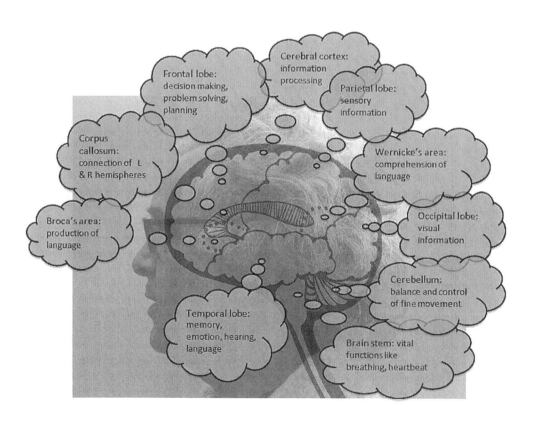

Harvey, thinking about thinking.

1
Why Did We Make This Movie?

Harvey Hubbell V

Well, I'm a filmmaker. The idea to make the film, *Dislecksia: The Movie*, first came up as my film team and I worked on a list of potential projects to do once we finished *Loop Dreams*.

I've done commercials, low-budget independent films, and high-budget features, but I lean toward social documentaries because they inspire people to think about something for ninety minutes. Commercials are film lies. Documentaries are film truths.

Harvey Hubbell V
Hawley School, Newtown, CT

Since I was a kid, I've felt misunderstood. In school, I wasn't trying to be a wise guy, and I wasn't being lazy. But no one understood then why I was acting like I was. Even I didn't understand until much later on that it was because my brain is wired differently, and I have dyslexia.

My major motivation to make this movie was to raise awareness in the general public, in policy makers, and even in dyslexics ourselves. I hope it can be a source of information and inspiration to get more teachers on board. Early on, I came to a chilling realization that it wasn't just my teachers, but so many other people's teachers who didn't get us. They just didn't understand that brains are wired differently. Why is that important? Because when students' brains are wired differently, it means that they learn differently. And teachers need to be trained differently to teach these different minds.

I have been married to this project since 2004. It started with a one-page treatment. But before I could put together a documentary on dyslexia, I had to set off on a quest to understand it really well myself. And it took a long time. Lucky for me, I have found an advantage in being dumber, rather than smarter in this world. When you're smart, you know it all and nobody can tell you anything. But if you're not smart, you have to look for answers.

I went to my first International Dyslexia Association conference in Philadelphia in 2004. I carried around a plastic brain to get people's attention, and when I had their attention, I described the project. Having already won some Emmys with previous films gave me enough credibility that people would talk to me about my intention to make the most comprehensive documentary on dyslexia ever.

Our film is totally independent. We are doing this without backers, but through our travels we began to find willing, interested, expert advisors. And they would give the names of other concerned people, and we built an advisory board. We started asking questions. Developing the research bank took about a year in itself. One of our big questions is *what is dyslexia?* If you start by asking that, you get a lot of different answers.

I think the best thing that's going to come out of this documentary and this book is awareness at many levels. Policy makers, parents, educators, and the general public will finally have an answer when a child who is having a terrible time learning to read asks, *What's the matter with me?*

The following is from a 2008 interview with Harvey and Eric Gardner, Producer and Editor of *Dislecksia: The Movie*, at the Sundance Producers' Conference, an annual summer event at the Sundance Institute in Utah.

Eric: People have been asking Harvey and me, "Why a story about dyslexia? It doesn't really seem to fit the mold of big impact documentaries. What drove you to tell this story?"

I'm not dyslexic, but Harvey is, and we're trying to change the world. That's a tall order, and I know a lot of people have tried before us, but what we're trying to do is to increase public understanding of dyslexia to influence changes in education so that more people can learn to read.

Harvey: Eighty-five percent of the prison population reads below a sixth grade level. Now that doesn't have to happen. We see it less as a learning disability, and more of a teaching disability. Teachers aren't getting the information they need to adapt their methods to better serve the needs of students with dyslexia.

Eric: That's the world-changing part. We think that if everyone in society knows how to read, then society will be a better place.

Harvey: Eric Gardner's one of the hardest working guys in show business, and puts in crazy hours. He is an editor in Los Angeles, currently working on *Survivor.* He would finish his job at whatever time, call me for the drive home, and while I would be blabbering on about the victories and defeats of the day, he would get home, fix something to eat, come to iChat, and there we'd go, starting another night's work. We've both been working a double shift for years. We have a good crop of interns working with us. I've worked with interns for eighteen years, and find it is crucial for this around-the-clock kind of work, where the only way to get it done is to get it done.

Why Did We Make This Movie?

Eric: Working on *Survivor*, I have been able to pick the brain of John Heard, the Post-Producer, who happens to be a genius. Before that, I worked with the original post-producer, Jen McClure, also a genius. They have been a great source of information, knowing the workflow, knowing the process. Having help and advice from such knowledgeable people has made this project fly.

Harvey: Making a good film is a lot like mountain climbing. We know we're going to the top, and we know where that is, but how are we going to get there? We try this, try that, try that, and just keep going. Both Eric and I expected to be home a little earlier with this project. It has been exhausting and demanding. We expected that it would be easier than it has been. But we want it to be the best it can be, so we spend the time it takes, and keep oiling the machine.

Eric: We editors shy away from directors who can't describe their own movie, or say, "Just edit something and when I see something I like, then I'll tell you." Harvey's one of those rare directors who can tell you just what it's supposed to be. So all I have to do is put the pieces together and we're good to go. Most of this movie Harvey explained to me in one crazy conversation three years ago: "We start with a little bit of me and my home movie footage, and then we weave in other dyslexics' experiences and brain experts with the latest scientific research. We include moms struggling with their kids, teachers who can make it work, and we end with a positive, uplifting message about the future of education."

When he told me this story with its inspirational ending, of course I thought he was nuts, and I didn't edit it in that order. Harvey looked at the first cut with the moms at the end and the education stuff buried in the middle and said, "It kind of feels like it needs to be, you know, more of an upper ending," and basically told me to put it back in his order. As an editor, I'm supposed to try different things, but you can't have so much hubris that when someone else is right, you continue to ignore it. You're still going to get the credit for editing anyway, so you should use the best idea, even if it wasn't yours.

Harvey: We're weaving a tapestry. We have located many people, some famous, some not, who have been evaluated and formally labeled with dyslexia. There are also the *alleged dyslexics*, famous folks in history whose work and life stories reveal classic characteristics of dyslexia, but whose struggle with words went officially unrecognized before the days of IDEA, IEPs, RTI, and BS. Albert Einstein's story, Thomas Edison's story, and quite a few more add a lot of texture and strength to the tapestry.

Eric: The other day we were on one of the local news shows with one of the scientists we had worked with... one of the top brain scientists in the world, president of the Haskins Lab at Yale University, *the* guy...

Harvey: ...and we wanted to show him what we had for the film before we went on the show together. Eric and I watched him and his wife as they were watching the cut, and we saw him writing down a question, and then another question, then another question, and we're thinking, *This is the litmus test.*

Eric: We're dying because he's writing down all these notes, and we're thinking, *Oh, we're screwed. He's gonna hate this thing.*

Harvey: So, he is watching this film where we are trying to be educational and entertaining at the same time – not so easy – but we know that when you laugh, a chemical is released in your brain and helps you remember better what you learned. But he must question what we have done because he is writing all these things down. Then, all of a sudden, he crosses one off. Then he crosses another one off. And he crosses another one off. Because... all of his questions are answered. *Exhale.*

Eric: We want to change the world. We want to change laws. We want to influence a real difference in education that can touch many lives, and we hope our film will be a conversation starter.

Eric Gardner and Harvey Hubbell V

2
Why Did We Create This Book?

Harvey Hubbell V

We've got a film, and we've got a book, and we've got friends to help us spread the word – that's multisensory. We would like to get our message out in different ways. Over the last several years, we were able to go out and meet all kinds of people, some of them leading brain researchers. I consider these folks the rock stars of dyslexia, and I figured if they would sit down and explain dyslexia in a friendly conversation with me, people like me might be able to understand it. We transcribed years of interviews into logs and compiled the logs into this book. Our ninety-minute documentary can only contain ninety minutes worth of information, but this book can provide a lot more of the great details and personal stories that couldn't make it into the movie.

Phyllis C. Orlowski, Parent, Teacher, and Co-Editor, *Dislecksia: The Book*

If one in seven people show signs of some form of dyslexia, why is it still a mystery to most? At the age of eight, Harvey was diagnosed with dyslexia, but his teachers didn't know how to address his learning difference. And today, more than 40 years later, the majority of our educational system still hasn't figured out how to effectively identify and teach children with dyslexia. Many people spend their entire lives struggling in a literate world, never knowing they have dyslexia.

As Harvey began filming for his movie, some of the people he encountered were mothers and fathers advocating for their dyslexic children. One of those mothers was me. We bumped into each other at our thirty-year high school reunion.

Although we grew up in the same town in Connecticut and went to the same public schools, our paths rarely crossed. I certainly was aware of Harvey throughout all of our years of school – it was impossible not to be. Harvey was a very visible student, a pack leader with a way of stirring up a crowd. He wore a jean jacket with *Pazzo* spelled out in brass studs on the back, a word that he found in a paperback about a gang of Italian street thugs. I avoided Harvey and his gang, the *Pazoos*, but couldn't help wondering; *what was with this guy? Why did he want to make life more difficult for the teachers and administrators at Newtown High School?*

I didn't realize how much we were all misinterpreting his cries for help.

My friends, who knew that I was defending my dyslexic son's right to an education and on the verge of suing my public school district for private school reimbursement, directed me to Harvey at the reunion. He had a new mission and was proudly promoting his latest movie, *Dislecksia: The Movie*, with a postcard that hung from a string around his neck. For the first time ever, after knowing Harvey for more than forty years, we had something in common.

It is not easy to comprehend dyslexia unless one has experienced it firsthand. When my intelligent, eager to learn, and creative son, Desi, was finally diagnosed with dyslexia in the fifth grade, he had been struggling in school for many years. Although I am a teacher in a public school with a master's degree in reading, my training did not prepare me to help my own son. Desi spent two unsuccessful years in first grade. The original first-grade teacher even commented on his report card: *It saddens me to see a child apparently unable to learn... I regret that I am unable to promote him to second grade.* I understand now that she was not trained to recognize the condition of dyslexia or teach a dyslexic student to read and write. Unfortunately, most teachers still do not have that training.

This began my parental advocacy. I was a single mom with three sons to raise, but I knew I had to fight for Desi's education. I was also fighting for the life of this frustrated boy who would cling to me when it was time to go to school, crying in the morning and at night; *there is no school for me!* He was angry. He was sad. He wouldn't eat. Often wrapping himself up in a black cape, he pretended he

Desi Gialanella

was a vampire. He felt lonely and isolated in his struggles at school, frustrated with the task of learning to read, write and spell.

After Desi received an evaluation outside of the school system, and was diagnosed as dyslexic, we finally had a name for his years of struggle. I devoured every book I could find and searched the Internet for information, strategies, and miracles. By sixth grade, he was barely reading at a second grade level, and his writing skills were even lower – but I had learned a lot. I learned that children in the United States should be protected under the Individuals with Disabilities Education Act (IDEA); that dyslexia is a Specific Learning Disability under IDEA 2004: I/A/602/30; that all children have the right to a Free Appropriate Public Education (FAPE); and that children should be protected through No Child Left Behind (NCLB) and Response to Intervention (RTI).

I made multiple requests for our district to send a teacher for training in a scientifically proven, Orton-Gillingham-based reading program.

When my requests were denied, I found the Gow School in South Wales, New York, a wonderful boarding school that specializes in teaching dyslexic boys. The Gow School was, alas, very expensive and far beyond my financial means. So, I hired a special education lawyer to represent Desi and sued my district for tuition reimbursement and legal fees. I felt there was no other choice.

Within weeks (weeks!) at Gow, Desi's self-esteem increased dramatically. He learned to *really* read, reaching a sixth-grade level by the end of seventh grade. He gained confidence, made new friends, played in sports programs and shed the vampire cape.

This was just seventh grade, and it cost me a second mortgage on my home and forced me to take on additional jobs sewing custom curtains, coaching high school tennis, and working at a B&B to afford it. I scraped by emotionally and financially, buoyed by Desi's continued growth in eighth grade. Even with a second mortgage and the extra jobs, I needed financial assistance from my father and substantial financial aid from The Gow School.

A New York State Education Impartial Hearing Officer (IHO) heard our case in the winter of 2007/8. At the end of five full days of hearings, my special education attorney and I left with a transcript of over one thousand pages of testimony from our district's special education director, teachers, school psychologists, and evaluators who admitted that my son's educational needs were neglected, and that he had not been classified as a child with a learning disability on a timely basis. It was revealed that they had ignored Desi's psychological cries for help in first through third grades and that they had proposed an illegitimate special education program within the regulatory construct of New York to commence in fourth grade. It was also proven that the district did not follow-through with their commitment to train two sixth-grade teachers in a scientifically proven, Orton-Gillingham based method. Furthermore, it was discovered that the school district had illegally taught two classes at the same time (breaking New York state special education laws); that they failed to provide special education while Desi was in grades four through six (at a charter Montessori school); and that they neglected to provide an updated Individualized Education Plan (IEP) prior to the beginning of sixth grade. My special education lawyer believed that we had presented a strong case and were in good shape to prevail for tuition reimbursement and legal fees paid by the district school.

I held my breath for months before hearing that the IHO voted in favor of the district. No! It couldn't be. I had done everything right. The system was supposed to protect me and my son and provide Desi with a proper education. Against the recommendation of my attorney, I appealed his decision on my own, pro se, and sent the case to the State Review Officer (SRO) of New York. My lawyer had warned me that it is almost impossible to turn around the decision of an IHO, and that the SRO would most likely go with the same decision of the IHO due to deference. Indeed, the appeal was dismissed.

But hey! Our school never recognized Desi's dyslexia. His teachers had no idea how to help him. How could I stop now? I appealed the decision of the SRO and took it to the next level. When children are not accurately diagnosed and given intense, early intervention, the learning gap usually never closes. They do not catch up to their peers. This was not easy to learn, but it drives me to keep pushing, not just for Desi but for all dyslexics.

I hired Andrew Cuddy's law firm to take on the case, and borrowed more against my house, putting myself into even deeper financial debt and at risk of losing my home. Andrew Cuddy, Esq. is the author of the *Educational Battlefield* and a fearless advocate for special education students and their educational rights.

Unfortunately, I also lost my appeal at the Northern District Court. Unable to pay for a lawyer again, I did a nationwide search for a pro bono lawyer and asked every single International Dyslexia Association (IDA) Branch by state for financial assistance. I came up with no lawyer and no money. I attempted on my own to appeal to the Second Circuit Court, but I made a technical error and lost again. I filed a Motion for Reconsideration to the Second Circuit Court, but that was also denied. It was difficult to accept my defeat when I was just one step away from the Supreme Court after four years of efforts and thousands of dollars spent on lawyer's fees. My hopes to help many dyslexic children, aside from my own, were crushed.

I have learned that the due process system is grueling and flawed in many ways – it's nearly impossible to prevail. Districts succeed as single families' finances become depleted. Sadly, litigation becomes a battle between parent and school attorney. Because of confidentiality issues, key information that reveals gaps in instruction and ineffective methods rarely gets back to the teachers who might then change their practice. A family faces financial ruin while a school district simply pays an attorney through a private insurance company, burying the expense and hiding it from the taxpayers whose own children may be the ones who struggle.

Districts use public funds to fight off a pesky parent like me instead of pouring it into teacher training that would positively affect the lives of so many children. Parents cannot join forces and start class action suits because they cannot learn of others in similar situations – there are confidentiality laws, such as the Family Educational Rights and Privacy Act (FERPA) laws. So a self-serving system has been created for the most part to protect the hearing officers, schools, and their lawyers. In the end, it is our children that suffer – they are our nation's greatest resource, yet their civil rights and rights to an appropriate education may be compromised.

Desi and Harvey's stories are like the stories of too many other dyslexics. A capable child begins school and finds their entire world suddenly turned upside down when they encounter failure learning to read, write and spell. Those children do grow up. What comes next for those who can't read or write at proper level?

After re-connecting with Harvey at our high school reunion, I realized I wanted to become more a part of his *Dislecksia: The Movie* project and asked if I could help with his book. Harvey agreed, and together with my colleague, Julie Costanzo, we created this book based on the years of interviews that were conducted for *Dislecksia: The Movie*.

My advocacy for dyslexics and dyslexia awareness has continued on other fronts as well. I created a group called Dyslexics Rights on Facebook, and on a daily basis connect with nearly 5,000 people worldwide sharing information, ideas, videos, and thoughts on dyslexia. I have discovered dyslexia advocate friends in Spain, Argentina, Brazil, France, England, Mexico, Venezuela, Italy, Canada, Chile, Iceland, Africa, and the Middle East. It is fantastic to see the information shared worldwide daily and our own dyslexia awareness and comprehension grow through social networks!

Desi is now graduating and his future looks bright! With the documentation from his neuropsychological testing in hand and the recommendations from his doctors, Desi has advocated for his own accommodations. Desi works hard and amazes many of his teachers with his brilliance. He recently completed the ACT test with accommodations of triple time, a quiet and separate location, and a reader – he scored in the top 97th percentile in the reading section. How is that for a kid who struggled to read for so many years? How many others have the same capability, but are not given the same chance to shine with appropriate advocacy and accommodations?

As I better understand Desi, I finally have some idea why Harvey acted the way he did throughout our school years, and I understand with greater depth who he is today. *Dislecksia: The Movie* comes at a time when the case for educational reform is compelling. With that reform comes a critical need for awareness and a better understanding of dyslexia. If one in seven children in America is dyslexic, and schools are not recognizing cognitive diversity, we have a big problem. *Dislecksia: The Movie* and *Dislecksia: The Book* will hopefully be a part of the solution.

Julie Costanzo Special Education Teacher, Co-Editor, *Dislecksia: The Book*

During my thirty-plus years in education, my priority has been helping the students who don't respond well to typical instruction. But I haven't always been a teacher. I also served as Director of Curriculum and Instruction for nineteen small, rural districts under one of New York State's Board of Cooperative Education umbrellas. After finally having enough of budgets and grants, mining data, and minding superintendents, I returned joyfully to the classroom, where my mission has been to reengage at-risk high school students, to help them see their own self-worth and the value of an education.

Many of my students spend time outside school in a world of generational poverty, drugs and alcohol, incarceration, and unanticipated pregnancy. They have known failure at school since their early grades. Our district has created a program to encourage them to stay in school as long as possible, offering a half-day to acquire social and technical job skills at internships in the community and a half-day to acquire basic academic skills in my classroom – all with the goal of preparing them to function successfully as independent citizens, voters, workers, and parents in the world beyond school.

My students are sophomores, juniors, and seniors. Some have earned zero high school credits. They are tough, defensive, and angry. They avoid successful kids and typical high school activities. They feel dumb and they hate school. But they come. I see in them an inner

Noah-Schlitt

desperation and (although well hidden) fleeting remnants of hope. I think they may believe me when I promise them that I will find a way for them to learn better, so they can use and show the intelligence we know is there, and will not live their lives as victims who respond to life's challenges with false bravado, aggression, or passive surrender.

They believe me because in my classroom, they have felt some success. For years, these students did not even take state assessments because, with their low attendance and achievement, the district felt it would have been a punishing ordeal for them. Instead, the district took the hit for their non-participation. No more. That remnant of hope has driven these kids to sit down with me and devote some serious effort to learning. Together, we looked at current research on brain differences. Ideas about alternate ways of teaching and learning resonated around Room 240 like bat radar. A number of my students have now passed state assessments.

However, some of them continue to struggle with reading, painfully droning through passages at the second-grade level. Reading has felt like torture for them for years, and I don't blame them for hating to do it.

During my teacher training, the standard platform was a meaning-based reading program with letter/sound correspondences and spelling rules taught incidentally. By realigning my teaching practices to atypical learners, offering them a rich diet of background knowledge, relevant activities, and respect for their learning styles and need for processing time, I have helped some find their strength as confident readers. But every year, I have a few students for whom this is not effective. As my understanding of brain function has deepened, I have come to realize that these students require something more.

A year into my own study of dyslexia, after looking at Orton-Gillingham research and practice, I concluded that bringing a multisensory, explicit, structured, and sequential reading program to my students would be a promising intervention. I spent a summer acquiring my first thirty hours of training, and last September, my four struggling readers and I began.

Accustomed to failure and suspicious of starry-eyed teachers, these young men needed first to buy in, so we started with the brain model that sits on our table. We talked pathways, white matter, and fMRI's. We discussed how a combination of auditory, kinesthetic, and visual techniques could create or strengthen brain circuits to enable them to read more accurately and fluently. We talked about how it might feel to understand and learn with pleasure, not pain.

Even though I had rewritten all the cutsie mnemonics to reflect a tough guy's taste, my students were still embarrassed to be seen using plates of sand, plastic screens, blending boards, and tapping pads. We kept the door closed and gave it a shot.

Cut to June. Of the four, one student continued his pattern of poor attendance and benefited very little, and three took off like rockets. They pounded red words into their forearms and remembered them. They learned how to break words into syllables, and they learned the sounds that combinations of letters make. They stopped wildly guessing after glancing at the first letter of any long word. They can't wait to pick it up again in the fall. A mother cried at an IEP meeting.

That's why I am working on this book. I came to an understanding of dyslexia late, near the end of my career in teaching. But I realize now how critical and essential this body of knowledge is for teachers to be able to reach all of their students. All teachers, all students.

I learned about Harvey's movie while my son Sam was working with him as an intern, and after I saw a rough cut, I knew I wanted to be a part of this project.

My teaching colleague, Phyllis Orlowski, and I combed through fifteen fat binders of transcribed interviews. We took out inappropriate jokes (sorry), conversational stops and starts, and straightened out and rewove the threads of ideas that tangled into amazing configurations when a person with dyslexia interviewed another person with dyslexia.

And regarding that phrase, we understand and honor that dyslexia does not define a person, and a dyslexic is much more than that label. But we're trying to get a flow going here, and while changing every reference to a *dyslexic* to the stodgier *person with dyslexia* is morally correct, it does get tedious to read. People with dyslexia call themselves dyslexics, so we mostly went with that.

While we're at it, here is the gender justification. Yes, people with learning differences come in both genders, and we just tried to mix it up with no hidden meaning behind our references to *him* or *her*.

What follow are not our words. We have just organized, compiled, edited, and clarified. If we have done our work well, we will be completely invisible throughout this book. Invisible, but passionately there.

3
What Is Dyslexia?

Dyslexia is a neurological, hereditary brain difference. And it persists because it carries with it certain benefits.
Diana Hanbury King

People on the Street,
What do you say?

- Dyslexia is when you can't sleep at night.
- It's when you say a word and the letters come out backwards.
- It's like dementia. You don't remember well.
- My brother-in-law is dyslexic, and he's the director of a bank, so it's whatever he has.
- It's where you can't read.
- It's a syndrome that you're born with, and sometimes it's hard for you to work because you get confused.
- It's a speech impediment.
- It's when words don't be coming out too much like they should, and you wonder, *What's wrong with that dude?*
- It's an eating disorder. No, I'm sorry. Dyslexia is not an eating disorder. It's when you get your words mixed up, back and forth. I apologize. I'm slightly dyslexic. Sorry.
- I work with a person who is dyslexic, and he had to teach himself. He's a scientist. We work in a crime laboratory.
- My brother has dyslexia, and he reads everything backwards and turned around.

- It's when you switch your numbers and your words.
- It's part of a disease, right? You can't read words right, and you have a problem with slowness. You can't really figure out what the words mean.
- It's getting the letters backwards in a word. I think I'm a little bit dyslexic.
- You know what? I think my son is dyslexic because he has a problem reading. And my daughter. She has *b's* and *d's* and *z's* and *2's* transposed all over the place.
- In my state, they just call kids learning disabled. They don't have dyslexia.
- It's a disability where your mind transposes and sees something differently than it's printed.
- It's where your mind switches words around so it looks like they're backwards.
- It's a kind of disease that children have. There's an interruption of the brain.
- Dyslexia's when your brain sees things backwards.
- I think maybe it's miswiring of the brain. The kids I teach who have it usually work harder than kids who don't.
- I probably have it right now because I'm really stressed.
- It's when somebody can read backwards, but they can't read normally.
- I think that's when you read words backwards. They appear mixed up on the page.
- I know it's about reading backwards, something about being backwards.

Pop Quiz #1

Reading is an _____ skill, unlike spoken language.

      a.   automatic
      b.   acquired
      c.   easy

(Answer at the back of the book)

Harvey,

What do you say?

This will not be an easy question for me to answer because I am a nonlinear thinker – I'm happy and proud to be one. I know we need both linear and nonlinear thinking to solve problems, but while I consider what dyslexia is, I'll probably take off with it and disappear around a few corners, though I promise I'll bring it back.

One important idea is that people cannot be the same: Nobody has the same fingerprints, twins don't have the same DNA, and none of us think the same way. In every aspect, we are somewhere on a spectrum, and that includes a reading, writing, and learning spectrum. Some of us are severely affected by dyslexia, and some of us are mildly affected, but I think all dyslexics look at the big picture. We do not connect the dots in order, but when we combine our holistic approach with that of an orderly dot-connector, together we can come up with some amazing solutions. In that way, I think the world needs all of us.

I don't like the word dyslexia. *Dys* means bad or faulty, and *lexia* means language. But I'm writing this, you're reading this, and we are communicating to some degree, so I think it's a *faulty* word. My language abilities were first evaluated when I was a kid, back in the '60s. No one was real familiar with that word then, and no one explained what it meant. Later, I was evaluated for the movie, and this was good because since the '60s, I had been afraid that I was really dumb. From the most recent testing, I learned a lot about myself and how I process information differently.

Noah Schlitt

I still can't spell dyslexia, I really can't. I can learn to spell a word, but then I immediately forget it, so I guess I don't really learn it in the first place. We make that point with the title of the movie, *Dislecksia*. So there's difficulty with rapid retrieval, and there's difficulty with chronological processing, and on my own personal spectrum, there is terrible spelling. I do read, and I love to read, but I read slowly.

And my math is also bad - very *dys*. No matter how much my teachers tried to drag me through math to some sort of understanding, I just didn't get it. And because I carried a calculator in high school, I was considered a troublemaker. *Ooooo*. That was one of my compensating mechanisms. Another compensation was, and still is, using my friends' brains. They help me out a lot. So, I'm dyslexic, I have dyscalculia, and I have dysgraphia, which means my handwriting is also bad. That's another story, but those three areas give me an awful lot of *dys*.

So, bringing it back, dyslexia was what I brought with me to school. *Dys* was what they did to me while I was an inmate.

McKenzie Renee Telatovich
The Hillside School, Macungie, Pennsylvania

My homeworke used to over welm me. I would criy and I would get realy mad at mysef. It would tacke me al nigh to finishe my home work. I could not go outside to play or due any sports. At Hillside, it was ezzer to read and I read my first chapter book in the middle of third grade. I also learned how to yous some tecnologe to help me read. Now I am a groomer, trainer and handler of animals.

Brain Specialists,
What do you say?

Sylvia O. Richardson, MD, Past President, Orton Dyslexia Society

Simply put, dyslexia is a learning disability. At the bottom of this language learning disability is that the dyslexic individual doesn't seem to have phonemic awareness. An average child recognizes, without knowing it, that a word is made up of different sounds. Later on, he learns that those sounds correspond to unfamiliar shapes or symbols – the alphabet. This is the alphabetic principle. Dyslexia is a life-long proposition. It doesn't go away, but it responds very well to appropriate teaching.

Gordon Sherman, PhD, Executive Director of Newgrange School and Education Center

Dyslexia is brain-based. Limited to the language domain and connected to an issue with short-term memory, it is a difference in processing information that affects the ability to learn to read, write, and spell. Dyslexia isn't affected by IQ, but can be affected by the environment if that environment is a classroom where a child is not being taught effectively.

Research that goes back to 1979 and 1980 was really important because, for the first time, our research community had evidence that the dyslexic brain looked different under a microscope. The arrangement of neurons was different: not abnormal, not pathological, but different.

If neurons are arranged differently, you process information differently, and if you process information differently, that can produce both a series of weaknesses and a series of strengths.

Ken Pugh, PhD, President and Director of Research, Haskins Laboratories

It's a difference and not a biomedical disorder, in my view. We treat the area where dyslexia is a deficit and honor the areas where dyslexia is a blessing.

Jeffrey Gilger, PhD, Associate Dean, Purdue University

Dyslexia is an unexpected inability to learn to read, write, or spell. There has been a great deal of research on how the brain functions, and we know that especially in the language areas of the left hemisphere there are differences between people who have dyslexia and those who do not. There has been a lot of discussion about those areas that deal with the cortex, that thin grey layer that everyone thinks of when they picture a brain. But studies have also looked at other structures beneath the cortex and in other parts of the brain like the cerebellum. People with dyslexia have differences in those areas as well, so it looks like dyslexic brains aren't just different cortically on the left side, but have other differences too, in terms of the way the brain hooks up, where the two hemispheres connect, the way the cerebellum works, and so on. This lends credence to the idea that there isn't a distinct single special gene that causes dyslexia - there probably are multiple factors.

My hypothesis has come to be that people with dyslexia are better described as having atypical brain development. The brain can be atypical in a number of different areas, and that doesn't necessarily mean you have disabilities; it can also mean you have special gifts.

Maria-Farrell

Philip Rubin, PhD, Senior Scientist and CEO, Haskins Laboratories

Dyslexia is a label for a pattern of behavior related to problems with reading, usually related to an inability to adequately break down spoken and written words into their component parts.

Ken Pugh, PhD, President and Director of Research, Haskins Laboratories

When reading lags behind other functions of the brain, such as memory, attention, language, math, and spatial reasoning, we consider that a fairly good signature of reading disability. Kids and adults who are struggling with reading generally fail to show the activation or organization in the left posterior brain, both in the temporal parietal and in the ventral pathway. What we often see in a number of studies is a tendency to use a very different set of pathways to read, involving the right hemisphere and also the frontal lobe areas that are involved in memory and other aspects of cognition, so this becomes a biomarker or a signature of dyslexia.

Gad Elbeheri, PhD, Executive Director, Centre for Child Evaluation & Teaching

I view dyslexia as a learning difference, not a disability. But perhaps I say that because of the law. In Kuwait, you must have a label to have an allocation of resources. So a label is not a bad thing. If the law says you are learning disabled, and with that you are entitled to go to a school that will help you, it's not a problem. But there are all sorts of points of strengths and points of weaknesses with the label of a learning disability. In the definition given by the British Dyslexia Association, they say that dyslexia is a combination of abilities and disabilities. They stress the fact that it is a combination of both, which is very good.

What Is Dyslexia?

Richard Olson, PhD, Professor, Colorado Learning Disabilities Research Center

When children are unusually slow in learning to read, and find reading really difficult at the beginning, in spite of good instruction, that is dyslexia. They might have a high IQ. They might have a low IQ. They might have attention deficit disorder. They might not. The key is that they are struggling in learning to read.

If I look at the state test scores of kids in Colorado, they follow a normal distribution or a bell curve. There are fewer kids the farther out you get on the low tail and fewer kids the farther out you get on the high tail of that distribution. Most people are kind of in the middle, and it is very continuous. There is no separate group that is uniquely dyslexic, bunched up like a lump at the end of the low tail. So dyslexia comes in gradations on a continuum. You could be in the second percentile of reading and be having a really hard time learning to read, or you could be in the tenth percentile and it is a little easier for you, but you are still behind most of your classmates. Even kids who are on the very low tail of the distribution, especially by the time they are in the higher grades, will certainly read if they've had good instruction. You might find a tenth grader reading at the fourth grade level, for example. That would put him at a very low percentile, but he is reading. It's just that his progress has been much slower compared to the average kid.

Christopher Faust
Churchill Center and School, St. Louis, Missouri

I lrnd to read betr in ttorel. My wrst thing before coming to Churchill wes I con not think and remember wrds.

Roger Saunders, Past President, International Dyslexia Association and helped found Jemicy School

Dyslexia is a neurologically based learning difference in language. It's not just a reading problem. From the Greek, the prefix *dys* means difficulty coping, and *lexia* means language, so dyslexia means difficulty coping with language in its many forms: reading, spelling, writing, speaking, listening, and so forth.

Carolyn Cowen, Executive Director, Carroll School Center for Innovative Education

Dyslexia varies greatly from individual to individual, not only in terms of the types of strengths and weaknesses, but also the degree.

Having dyslexia doesn't mean you're going to be tremendously gifted in some particular area, but it does seem to me, from rubbing shoulders with dyslexics all the time, that there is a disproportionate amount of strengths and talents in certain areas, such as the visual-spatial areas. That is why, in the field, we talk a lot about the strengths and weaknesses in every child.

Einar Mencl, PhD, Senior Scientist, Haskins Laboratories

In the brain, an area in the occipital temporal cortex and another part up front called Broca's area need to talk to each other. This is a given within the physiology of reading. What we see is that good readers do not show strong relationships between these areas when they are young, but as they get older, at twelve or thirteen years of age, these two areas go up and down in activation together, and we see a developmental shift toward these two areas communicating when kids read.

In the brains of both younger and older readers who have dyslexia, these two areas do not correlate with each other.

Ovid Tzeng, PhD, Professor, National Yang-Ming University

As a cognitive scientist, I am interested in dyslexia because written language is at the heart of civilization. Does dyslexia exist in Chinese? I'd say it is language-universal, very rooted biologically. In my research, I see that the aspect of sound is important for reading Chinese, even though it is not an alphabetic language. In terms of the brain locations that support this dynamic, I believe they are similar across all languages.

Tomi Guttorm, PhD, University of Jyväskylä, Finland

Dyslexia exists also in Finland. In the Finnish language, we have quite a regular system where one single letter is pronounced in one way, so it makes it very easy for beginning readers. We see differences in brain activations similar to those we see in English speakers with dyslexia. But Finnish dyslexics usually have more problems with fluency than with accuracy.

The Finnish government is funding a lot of research related to helping children with dyslexia early, even before they are in their first grade. I have spent the last ten years studying dyslexia, and I am convinced that it is not about laziness, and it is not about stupidity. It is a specific problem dealing with combining letters with sounds that has an effect on people's lives.

Guinevere Eden, PhD, Past President, International Dyslexia Association

Warren Asplen

It is important to understand the relationship between a language and its writing system. When we think about the identification of children with dyslexia and the avenues of treatment, it is important that we don't just focus on English, and more importantly, that we don't just focus on the alphabet. Once we start looking at languages and cultures where the writing system is different, we find differences in the dyslexic profile. If we look at scans of children in China who have dyslexia, the areas that are affected in the brains of those children are different from the areas that are affected in our English-speaking children.

That's not surprising, but we need to think about this when we design interventions that can be beneficial to children all around the world.

Gad Elbeheri, PhD, Executive Director, Centre for Child Evaluation & Teaching

Even though they may speak very different languages, underlying cognitive problems are more or less similar for all people with dyslexia. Cross-language studies have enriched our understanding of this, and work on dyslexia in German, Arabic, Hebrew, and Greek languages, for example, is ongoing.

One of the things we have been looking at in Arabic speakers who struggle with reading is whether the issue is reading accuracy, comprehension, or rate. According to our research, accuracy of reading in Arabic is usually easier than in English because Arabic is a more straightforward language with more one-to-one correspondence between what you say and what you write. So we can identify someone who is dyslexic in Arabic by measuring the time it takes to read a passage.

Ken Pugh, PhD, President and Director of Research, Haskins Laboratories

Although Chinese, English, Finnish, and Italian differ in many important ways, kids tend to develop common neural pathways to support fluent reading in these languages, and those with developmental dyslexia show largely overlapping areas of brain differences. This is an active research question with no final answers.

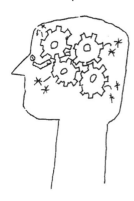

Warren Asplen

The fact that dyslexia tends to co-occur with other challenges such as ADHD or specific math disability doesn't mean that they have a common mechanism. One hypothesis is that if you have one or the other as your core neurobiological challenge, it could kind of spill over and make you look as if you had the other one. For example, if you were severely dyslexic, you might have so many difficulties socially and in school that you would begin to show symptoms that mimic ADHD without having the true neurobiological mechanism. Or if you have ADHD, it might be difficult to focus on reading. We have co-morbidity of these conditions, but we need more research to find a full explanation.

Guinevere Eden, PhD, Past President, International Dyslexia Association

Wherever you look in the literature, you see a slightly different emphasis when people describe the kinds of difficulties that kids and adults with dyslexia face. Those different emphases have driven different paths of research. Sometimes it's overwhelming when you attend scientific presentations at a conference on dyslexia. You hear some presenters talking about the motor system, some talking about auditory processing, some talking about the visual system, or some talking about just reading.

The reason is that individuals with dyslexia do have a variety of different behavioral manifestations. They're different. They have some common difficulties in terms of reading, but as individuals, they are all different from one another. As researchers, that's something that we have to keep in mind. We're not looking at one type of person. We are looking at children with a variety of differences that contribute to their reading problems, and we need to understand all of these in order to be most effective.

Ken Pugh, PhD, President and Director of Research, Haskins Laboratories

Dyslexia is not a life sentence; it's a learning difference. I don't judge it as bad or good but do understand that those areas where it creates real challenges academically are potentially treatable. Most importantly, we have evidence that kids' brains are highly plastic, capable of tremendous amounts of learning and change, and the evidence coming from controlled and careful intervention studies suggests that very large numbers of kids can really be positively affected by good evidence-based instruction. Above all else, we need to find the earliest markers that help us find kids and know who they are before they fail in literacy, so that we can be doing prevention rather than intervention.

Gordon Sherman, PhD, Executive Director of Newgrange School and Education Center

There are two important pathways for getting information into long-term storage in the brain. One is through what's called the phonological loop, or verbal short-term memory. That's typically how we are asked to learn in school. We read, we listen to a teacher, and that information gets into short-term memory, and then is consolidated into long-term memory. That's one very strong pathway for learning, but we know it is inefficient at best in people with dyslexia. That is why it is difficult for them to remember the sounds that compose words, and that could be a prime reason for problems learning to read. The second major pathway for getting information into the brain is the visual-spatial sketchpad. We understand this less well, but I like to think of the visual-spatial sketchpad as a big whiteboard on which you can put numbers and letters and manipulate them. It is not a good way to remember words or sounds, but it is a good way to remember visual images and to think in terms of imagery. It is a good way to solve very complicated problems because you can manipulate high-level concepts.

I believe that if you have really good language skills, your spatial skills are not quite as good. I think there's a negative correlation between the two. And I would suggest that the visual-spatial sketchpad is a strong way for people with dyslexia to get information into the brain.

We know people with dyslexia learn things. They're very proficient in life after school as long as they haven't been damaged too much by their school experiences. If you don't have an effective phonological loop, it is hard to get information into the brain in a way that allows you to be a good reader. But the visual-spatial sketchpad provides access to information that would allow you to be a good athlete, a good artist, and a good conceptual thinker.

It is not a form of thinking that is stressed in school, however, and is not a major part of instruction except in gym class. So if you are a soccer or baseball player, along with your motor skills, you are using your visual-spatial pathway. In general, teachers don't have strong skills in this area because they are usually selected for their strengths in the other pathway. Our educational system has not yet designed an effective curriculum for students who learn best in this visual-spatial domain.

Robbie Tonner

Dyslexia is a prime example of cerebrodiversity, and that is a good thing. If all of us were the same, there would be challenges to our species in the environment, whether viral, bacterial, or cognitive, that we would not be able to overcome. We need a lot of variation so that when the challenges come around, there will be people with a different kind of immune system that can fight the virus or people with a different kind of brain that can figure out the challenge of a toxic Earth. Cerebrodiversity is key for the survival of humans. There is no one best way to answer a question, and nature understands that. And so does the business world. If you put a lot of different people together on a project, you're going to get your best result. In a sense, that's why we are a successful species, because we have all those differences. If we try to reduce those differences, whether through genetic manipulation or environmental manipulation, that limits those team members who can bring diverse processing to an attempt to answer a question.

Tess Crocker
Eagle Hill School, Greenwich, Connecticut

In my previous schools, I went through a series of seemingly endless moments of being misunderstood, of being punished and laughed at for things I had no control over. But at Eagle Hill, I

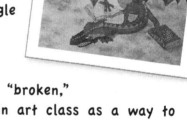

wrote an essay describing how I see the world, and how the world, in telling me that I am "broken," suffers. I created the dragon in art class as a way to leave something of myself at EHS.

Dyslexics,
What do you say?

Dana Blackhurst, Headmaster, Camperdown Academy

I'm not that efficient at reading and writing. I'd like to be better at it, but I have other things to do.

Olivia Hanson, Graduate, The Forman School

I have a learning difference. Disability sounds kind of mean. I don't like that word. I'm different but in a good way. I learn best by seeing. If someone is explaining something to me, it helps me understand it if I can have a little drawing or picture in front of me. Then I can picture it because my imagination is very vivid. It is more difficult for me if someone is just talking. Here in Costa Rica, we were doing pitfall traps, and I didn't understand how they were supposed to be set up until someone drew it out on a piece of paper. Then it became clear. Perfectly clear.

Billy Bob Thornton, Musician, Actor, and Filmmaker

A lot of people think that with dyslexia you turn your letters around backwards, that kind of thing. They have a simple understanding of it, and say, "Oh yeah, I've got that. I always put my right sock on first." But I'm like, "Honey, you have no idea," because for some of us, the complexities of it are astounding. It is much more complicated, and for most of my life, it's been pretty painful.

Some people even laugh at you when you tell them you have dyslexia because they don't consider it a big deal, "Oh, so my name's really Wilson Ron, right?" That's real funny. I don't think they understand exactly how it affects you. For me, it's exhausting. It actually depletes your energy. If I have to read something, at the end of it I'm ready to go to bed with a headache.

What Is Dyslexia?

To this day, reading is painful for me. I don't read well, and to top it off, I guess I have ADD. As an actor, I learn my dialogue for movies by having people read it to me. I don't learn it off the page. But I do retain what I read if I am interested in it. I read the same books over and over because I know them and love them. And I can speed-read and get the facts about something, but I miss the nuances. I have to read slowly to understand the nuances. It takes me a long time to get through five pages.

Tom West, Author

Thomas Edison kept a diary for several months when he visited the original Chautauqua, an educational, cultural summer retreat for adults. He wrote about his experience with a roomful of people playing parlor games: he finished at the very bottom of the group and failed at all the memory games. This is a typical dyslexia story.

Sarah Spier, Founder and President of Mwambao Alliance, Mwambao Primary School, Tanzania

Instead of labeling it, I think it's more important to talk about what we can do about it. And what is a disability? Because we can't do math as well as someone else, because we can't read as well, because we read slower, that makes us disabled? But what about the people who can't do art as well as us, or who can't think of things the way we do, or who can't do film work, they're not called disabled. Why not?

Sarah Joy Brown, Emmy Award-winning actress

Dyslexia is just the way I see and hear everything, filtered through what the world wants to call a learning disability. To me, it is just the way I function, and I can't imagine any other way.

Joe Pantoliano, Emmy Award-winning actor

I have learned how to read, and I don't see words backwards, but I do get things mixed up sometimes. Mornings when I am out of town are the worst, when I dial my home phone number and get somebody I don't know at somebody else's house.

David Boies, Attorney, *Time* magazine's 100 Most Influential People in the World in 2010

I didn't read until I was in third grade, but this was in the 1940s, in a small, Illinois farming community. Reading wasn't the highest goal for a young boy at that time, and no one I knew was aware of the term dyslexia or associated it with slowness in reading. I always knew that for me, reading was harder to do than lots of other things, but I really didn't pay much attention to it. Our first two children did not have learning disabilities, but when my next two children, fraternal twins, were ready for school at about five or six years old, one was extremely verbal and read very easily, and one had extraordinary difficulties and could not read at all. When we took him to a couple of testing centers to try to understand why there was this obvious difference, the experts explained his learning disability, and then took a look at me and diagnosed me as well.

Kylie Mckee

By that time, I had been through school and was practicing law, so I really didn't focus as much on my own difficulties as on the pain and uncertainty that parents have when they discover that their child is going to have a harder time than other children.

I think it was a lot easier for me growing up with dyslexia than it is for children today. I was slow in reading, but others were slow in math or social studies. I could do a lot of my work by listening, memorizing, and looking for pictures, so it really wasn't much of a stigma for me. When I was growing up, people were given time to develop. They were given time to overcome obstacles, and they were given space where their obstacles did not make them feel uncomfortable, inadequate, or as one of my children with dyslexia said, *stupid*.

But I did have to learn how to read. I never learned to read very well and still don't. It takes me a long time to get through a page. But I had to learn to read well enough that I could understand it. And I also had to learn how to learn without reading, by paying attention. I listened a lot in class. I didn't take many notes because it was hard for me to listen, absorb, and take notes. But I learned that I could learn by listening, and I was able to do that in college, and I was able to do that in law school.

I learned to adapt to certain requirements of college reading by skimming, finding the key points, and really learning those. One advantage of reading slowly is that you do focus on every word and you do remember things.

I have one portal, reading, that is partially blocked. When I use that portal, I have to operate less efficiently and more slowly than I would otherwise. It doesn't affect my processing once I get information into my system, but I have an input problem. I'm a computer system with a faulty optical character recognition system. But it's not crippling because I believe that input is the least important of the functions of thinking and analysis, and there are lots of ways around it.

Stephen J. Cannell, Writer, Producer

Some people have terrible problems with some of this stuff and no problem at all with other parts of it. But one difficult area for some dyslexics is sequencing. You say to a dyslexic, "Go upstairs, pack up your school books, make sure your history paper is in there, turn off the lights in your bathroom and come down." And the kid will think, *Go upstairs, pack my... what was the next one?* The whole idea of holding on to a sequence of events can be very difficult.

It is interesting that people who do not have this condition do actually experience a similar frustration when someone comes to their table at a restaurant and they've known him their whole life, but they can't pull his name up. Dyslexics have that same difficulty at school on tests when they have something in their memory, but they just can't pull up the file.

Sarah Joy Brown, Emmy Award-winning actress

My brain is not set up to work like most people's, although I try to go by their rules as much as possible. But I can't email. That's just a nightmare with so many numbers and letters and things coming at me. It's like pulling my teeth to get me to read a plain email where there is nothing to recognize and to email somebody back. But Facebook, where half of the same information is visual, makes perfect sense to me, and I really thrive in that environment.

Billy Bob Thornton, Musician, Actor, and Filmmaker

The good news is that as a writer and as a songwriter, I can sit down and write stuff. People can't read it, but at least I can write it down. They have tried to teach me to type, but if everything's out of order in my head already, and you give me a keyboard where everything's out of order again, you got me. I can't type or work a computer at all. So I always write by hand, with a pencil. Most of the things I write are done automatically, in a stream of consciousness. I just start writing and let the thing take me where I go. The problem with that is that I write things backwards and out of order, and I leave words out all the time and it's not like, *Oh, you'll never be able to read my writing; here let me read that for you.* With me, even I can't read my writing.

To get somebody to be able to type up my screenplay, I have to go through it all again and figure out what the hell I just wrote. Mostly, I just remember it from the story I have in my head. My assistant and I will go through a screenplay to correct it, and I'll say, "Oh no, that's not right," because sometimes I have people talk weird, saying things strangely or out of order. So she never knows if it's my dyslexia that caused the strange wording or if it's really the way the person talks. She has to go through it with me and ask me, "Did you mean to do this or not?" I tell her that I meant to do this one, didn't mean to do that one, meant to do this one, and that's how I write.

Keaghan Hamilton, Graduate of The Forman School

We don't see something backwards, we just comprehend it backwards. It gets lost in our brain. It might go in the right way, but when we try to say it, it gets switched around. Reading takes me a while. I'll either just take my time, or I'll read with a friend and we'll switch on and off because I read faster out loud. I'm so used to what I do; I don't even think of it as compensating. It's just what I do. I never think of it as, *Oops, that's the wrong way.*

Simon Shankweiler
The Academy in Manayunk, Philadelphia, Pennsylvania

I am an artist, and one thing I feel particularly proud of is that I raised thousands of dollars for Obama by selling hot cocoa and my Obama Donkey buttons and t-shirts during the campane. I even got to hang out with Barak Obama! I did like my classroom teacher at my old school, he rocked! My resorse room teacher was always kind to me. But I always felt left out when I had to go down with two other kids from my class. It made me always wonder what I would be missing while I was gone.

At the Academy at Manayunk, I don't have to see a resorse teacher. All of my teachers teach me right in my class. My school is arts-based. I learn best this way. I wish that other kids who learn differently could have the great experience that I get to have at my school.

Billy Bob Thornton, Musician, Actor, and Filmmaker

Beyond the written page, I also look at the world differently, so maybe dyslexia doesn't only have to do with reading; maybe it has to do with the way you see and think about everything. I find that I am explaining myself a lot to people, "Can't you see that? Can't you see it that way?" And they're like, "No, I don't see it that way." My father's description for the way I think was *left-handed*.

Malcolm Alexander, Sculptor

It all began for me in 1988 when I learned I was dyslexic. What a relief. It was accidentally done. I was planning a seminar with a woman who instructed young people with learning difficulties. We were both artists. We were going to do the seminar, but we never could get the schedule figured out.

I said, "Why can't we figure this out?" And she said, "Because we're dyslexics." I said, "We're what?" She looked at me and said, "Malcolm, do you mean to tell me that you don't know you're dyslexic? Well, you're clinical. You're clinical, Malcolm." I said, "What do I do?" She said, "You go home this evening, mix a big martini, sit down, put your feet up, and say, here's to dyslexia!"

So that's how I learned I had it. I've never had the tests. I wouldn't do that. I don't do tests. I don't get past the directions.

I sat down and wrote a letter to Phillips Exeter Academy, where I had some very bad years. I realized that at that period I had a lot of anger within me. I was a very fine athlete, but boy, was I mean out there on the field. I played fullback. I loved to run in the line and knock someone down. It felt so good. Academically, it was a bust.

A war came along, and I went into the Marine Corps. I came out of the war with a disability. I had thought I was going to be the world's best athlete. That was over. The only thing left was academia, and I wandered my way into college and wandered my way out, went into the business world, got a wife, wasn't very successful.

One day, I woke up and said, *Hey, Malcolm, stop listening to other people. What's inside you?* I became an artist, and my self-esteem began to grow. I found that as I became a successful artist, I became a successful human being.

Aaron McLane, Special Effects Artist

I don't let dyslexia be a crutch. I just let it be what it is. *Oh, I'm sorry I miswrote that. I'm sorry I took your notes down wrong. I'm sorry I miswrote your phone number. Yeah, I'm dyslexic, and I wrote that wrong, but whatever.* Move on.

Sarah Joy Brown, Emmy Award-winning actress

I've had some embarrassing experiences. While shooting something for work, if they ask if I can read something off the teleprompter, I have to say, "Actually, no, I can't. I'll do it, but you're not going to like it. Trust me, get another actor to do it because I'll do it wrong a million times, and we'll be here all day." That can be embarrassing. So can those marriage vows. I'll memorize page after page on *General Hospital* without a problem, until I have to be married again. I've been married a lot on the soap, but I absolutely cannot remember wedding vows. I have to tape them to my co-star's chest every time.

It's always embarrassing for me to go to my daughter's school and be asked to sit down with the other parents and write on a piece of paper what she is allergic to and any kind of medical instructions. Any time I'm given a pencil and asked to write anything more than my name, I'm in an absolute panic because I can't spell. And there may very well be a doctor to my left or my right who can't spell either. I have a dear friend who's a neurologist and incredibly dyslexic and was told he was retarded as a kid. He eventually went on to be the head of pediatric neurosurgery at Children's Hospital in San Diego.

Lauren Retallick

So I try to tell myself that just because the person next to you is a doctor or a lawyer or some other professional who is really book smart and an amazing speller and may be about to judge you, you don't know how her brain works. You really don't know how she got through school. Just do your very best. Look for the gifts that you have because of what your brain does, and stop focusing on the things that it doesn't do. That kind of thinking helps to get me out of my own way.

Annette Jenner, PhD, Assistant Professor, Syracuse University

I had years of struggling in school. In kindergarten, I wrote my whole name backwards. The teacher said I'd outgrow it. In first grade, my reading level fell below grade level. They said I'd catch up. In second grade, I started in special education. In fifth grade, I was tested and given the label of dyslexic. In junior high, I really had problems, both academically and socially. By freshman year in high school, I was put on a non-academic drug. I was being taught how to fill out checks and job applications for McDonalds. When I'd ask my special education teacher why I had to continue to do this work, she said that it was to prepare myself for life after high school. I told her I was going to go to college. She told me that maybe I should consider that college was not for me. I had been thinking about college ever since I was five years old. That summer, I came to the Forman School and succeeded academically for the first time.

Labels are funny things – we all have more than one. Yes, I have the dyslexia label, but I also have the labels of professor, daughter, scientist, sister, teacher, wife, and mother. Labels are just something that describe one aspect about ourselves.

Delos Smith, Senior Economist for the Security Executive Council

I had severe learning challenges as a young child. I had very delayed speech, I could not learn to read, and I had terrible problems with left-right orientation. During second and third grades, I had fifteen months of an Orton program with a phonics approach, and in September of 1944, I was declared normal! I was cured! I entered fourth grade as a normal boy. They had reversed my orientation to left-right, and I could speak somewhat clearly. But this was a big mistake. I was far from normal.

I did start reading newspapers. I remember the first newspaper I ever read was the *New York Times*. I was reading very, very well. But you simply don't catch up with this language in fifteen months without any follow-through, and we never went back, which was a great shame.

The program may have given me some building blocks, and I may have started to use them to build a foundation, but it would have been so helpful to have been able to continue with Orton a while longer. I was one of the lucky ones to get some skills, but there was a lot more work that could have been done to make my path easier. This was strictly for reading, writing, and speaking. No one addressed my social problems. I never thought I would fit in with friends, and that was not even discussed.

My father was a journalist, and reading was important in our family, so I spent a lot of time practicing. I'm actually competitive in the left hemisphere world. But I always had a problem with talking, and it was very easy for me to slip backwards.

I had such rhythm problems. I was almost thrown out of ROTC. At Colorado College, Armed Forces Day is a big deal. At that time the president of Colorado College was a retired army general. He was on the bandstand with all of his fellow generals to watch twenty-five thousand soldiers march by, and there was one boy who was out of step the whole way. He was so angry, he went to the sergeant running the ROTC program and accused me of ruining the march deliberately. My sergeant said, "Oh no, he just can't march." It is a cliché but true that society doesn't like it if you are out of step.

I went to the Arthur Murray Dance Studio, where they practically guarantee they can to teach you how to dance. After three or four hours of dancing with me, they gave me my money back, and I had to promise that I would never tell anybody that I went there, because they didn't want anyone to think they had taught me to dance the way I did. I was just out of step in so many ways.

So, from age nine, when I had my fifteen-month program and was supposedly no longer *dys-lexic*, to age forty-one, when something very special happened on December 9, 1976; I had a condition that I call *neutral-lexia*. Yes, I could read now. I could write now. I had a decent job, and I could compete in this society, but there were a lot of things about me that were still quite different.

In 1970, I had gone to music school because of my problem with dancing. I was a very good athlete and still could not understand why I couldn't learn to dance when I excelled at many sports. How could I throw a bowling ball so accurately and not be able to dance? How could I be an excellent baseball pitcher and not be able to dance? I just couldn't understand this about myself, although I knew my family wasn't particularly musical. And so I thought music lessons might help me. I was awful. I kept at it though, and then came the great day of December 9, 1976 when I played *Oh, My Darling Clementine* completely backwards (meaning from the right side of the page to the left, and from the bottom of the page to the top). I got my first musical feeling. Oh my God, there it was!

There are a whole series of questions that I have never really tried to really tackle about the language difficulties I had as a youngster. I didn't understand it. I didn't even know what the word dyslexia was. But when I did start to understand it, I started on the path from *dyslexia* through *neutral-lexia* to *plus-lexia*.

On December 9, 1976, I reverted to writing everything backwards, right to left. If I had any choice in this, I would never write in the usual way, from left to right again, because to me that feels backwards, and my way feels like writing forwards. But nobody understands this.

Because of my past experience, I considered myself an Orton person, and because I was also good in finances and had become a federal budget expert, I became the treasurer of the New York branch of the Orton Society. And that gave me a chance to meet the experts.

I met very famous neurologists like Dr. Norman Geschwind, who took a great interest in me. I was afraid that the question on my mind was a stupid one, but I asked Dr. Geschwind anyway, "Why can't I drink alcoholic beverages?" He immediately drew me a picture of the brain stem in the back of the head. He didn't think my question was stupid at all, and said, "Of course you can't drink! You'll lose your language. Everyone loses their language after drinking a certain amount of alcoholic beverages. But you'll lose language with three drops because of where your language center is."

So many people never learn these things, but ever since I did, I have called myself *plus-lexic*. I learned to take the anger out. I learned to depersonalize my differences because this is just how society operates. It is not against me, personally. I have to accept it or not, and think of strategies to help myself fit in and function in a society that was not designed with me in mind. It doesn't help to be angry all the time.

It comes back to the most elementary Greek philosophy from thousands of years ago, *Know yourself*. And we don't know ourselves. It is simply amazing to me that we don't teach school children about their brains. In my economics classes, which have nothing to do with dyslexia, I give lectures to students about their brains because they need to understand who they are. No matter what field they are in, they need to know how to maximize their strengths and compensate for their weaknesses.

Sarah Bernecker
Hamlin Robinson School, Seattle, Washington

I didn't understand things at school. My teachers tried to help, but they didn't understand. They kept moving on to new things. I am overjoyed that I am now at a school where I can actually learn. Being able to understand is a dream come true. And I love to compete in ballroom dancing. Dancing allows me to express myself physically, not mentally.

Teachers,

What do you say?

Joyce Pickering, SLC/CCC, CALT, QI, Hum D, Executive Director Emeritus of Shelton School

I've heard many times, *Oh, his spelling is fine. He got 100 on his test on Friday.* But can he spell those words two days later in an email to Grandma? He may not be really spelling the way most children do, he may be memorizing frantically. This goes on until about the third grade, when parents may fear that their child just isn't trying, isn't motivated, and his teachers aren't very good. The teachers may say that the home situation isn't very organized, and there is an emotional problem. And most of the time, it is none of these things. It is a neurobiological difference called dyslexia.

Arlene Sonday, Founding Fellow and first President of the Academy of Orton

Dyslexia is the inability to read, write, and spell. We used to think it was a visual issue, but actually it is language-based. It occurs in people who are very bright, as well as in those who aren't. Some very, very creative people have dyslexia. If you catch children early enough, they will be able to rise above it and meet whatever aspirations they have. Many people think it's awful to have dyslexia, but really, if you can teach kids to read and write adequately, they can go anywhere and do anything they want.

Some children have trouble organizing. Some have motor problems. Some have speech and language issues. Some have difficulty with semantics and syntax, word order, and grammar when they are speaking. Others have articulation problems. They might say /w/ for /r/, and when they speak that way, it makes a difference in the way they perceive and spell words. Some children have trouble with retrieval and can't remember a word. They'll look at a picture of a comb and they'll say, "It's... um, um..." They're working on it, they're acting it out, but they can't come up with the name of the object.

Some have trouble sequencing. They have trouble isolating sounds, and this is why we have them segment the sounds of a word with their fingers, tapping the sounds or writing them in the air, so they will be able to write the letters in the right order.

On top of that, we have attention deficit disorder or attention deficit hyperactivity disorder, two other areas where children can't seem to focus well enough to retain information and get it into long-term memory. Now all of these issues, all of the dyslexia, dyscalculia, dysgraphia, can go from mild to severe, and they can be co-morbid or exist together. You can have two of them, or five, or any combination, and it is a tough job to determine which ones are severe, which are mild, and which ones to attack first.

Then to add to the problem, if you are working with children who are in fifth or sixth grade or above, there is an emotional overlay. Because they have experienced difficulty for so long, they act up or withdraw, and there is a behavior issue.

Evelyn Russo, PhD, Haskins Laboratories Literacy Initiative

Before you are a beginning reader, before you can lift the word off the page, three things have to happen: you need to be able to hear sounds in a word, you need to have an idea of the alphabetic principle, and you need to have a concept of word. We were never wired to read or write. We were wired to speak.

In reading, the brain has to do something it never had to do before: think about words as being made up of sounds. Before the ability to read develops, a table is just a table, a cat is just a furry little creature. Meaning is attached to these words. But now we have to begin to think about the sounds of these words. Our brains are designed to receive these sounds in an acoustic bundle, so they are difficult to separate. The brain has to process and separate things that were always meant to be together, until the alphabet was invented.

Nancy Cushen White, EdD, Associate Clinical Professor and Learning Disabilities Specialist

Dyslexia is a language learning disability that may affect oral language, written language, decoding, spelling, listening, vocabulary, comprehension. The weakness that has been most researched and most confirmed is phonological. Some students can memorize words well enough to get by, but they have no idea why the words are pronounced a certain way, so they can't use that information for spelling.

It is a myth that people with dyslexia see letters or words backward. They don't. They see things the way everyone else does. This is a cup. I can turn it, and it is still a cup. And turned another way, it is still a cup. Turn a *b* and a *d* and a *q* and a *p* different ways, making minor changes in how they look, and they take on different names and make different sounds.

Dyscalculia is difficulty with calculation in math. I see many students who have no difficulty with math concepts, but they have a hard time with the language and symbols of math. For instance, there is a processing speed test where you look across a row of numbers to find the two that match. When the numbers have one digit, it is not so difficult. But when the numbers have two and three digits, sequencing difficulties arise, just as with letters and sounds, and it takes some students a much longer time to be successful.

Dysgraphia is specific to handwriting. If a student has difficulty with the mechanics of handwriting, then all the effort going into the act of writing is going to diminish the ability to formulate thoughts and spell them correctly. Keyboarding can be an alternative, but the myth of keyboarding, *Just put them on a keyboard, and they will be fine,* is that if typing is not automatic, the same problem of competing mental efforts will arise.

Diana Hanbury King, Founder of The Kildonan School

Dyslexia is a neurological, hereditary brain difference. And it persists because it carries with it certain benefits. A famous example of this phenomenon in the hereditary realm is sickle-cell disease, which carries with it immunity to malaria.

Naomi Adrianne Royster
Friendship School, Eldersburg, Maryland

When I was at a public school, we took a really big test that I had to take by myself. No one read the questions to me, so I just guessed. I have learned how to read better here at Friendship School. My teacher taught me how to sound out and read more. Now I am more fluent when I read. This is my masterpiece, an abstract representation of myself.

Dyslexia Advocates,

What do you say?

Linda Selvin, Project Director, Consultant at Energy One

Dyslexia is a neurologically based learning difference that results in difficulties in areas such as accurate letter recognition, fluency, and spelling. It is important to find out exactly where the difficulty is. Is it letter-sound recognition? Word recognition? Is there a hearing issue? A vision issue? People really need to have a specific diagnosis, and so they go through a battery of tests. Only a professional who understands learning disabilities should be doing the evaluation.

No two dyslexics are the same. Some are great verbally. Others aren't. Some have phenomenal memories and great recall. Others don't. Dyslexia comes in all sizes, shapes, and degrees. It can be very mild or quite extreme in the way that it affects a person's life.

It is a fallacy that there are more boys than girls with dyslexia. I remind educators that there has been no proof that more males have dyslexia. Because a boy with dyslexia may be more likely to act out, and a girl may tend to stay quietly in the back of the classroom, it is important for teachers to know how to interpret the behavior of boys versus the behavior of girls.

Carol Hill, Parent and educational advocate for dyslexics

I didn't know what dyslexia was until I encountered it with my children, and I think a lot of people have the same story. Then, as adults, we find we also have dyslexia. I have come to learn that our brains are hardwired for speech, but they are not hardwired to read, write, and spell – that's a skill. And you could be good at that skill or not good at that skill, just like fence building. Only, you can take or leave building fences, but you must develop some skills in reading, writing, and spelling. So dyslexia is a weakness in that area, although we may have a lot of strengths in other areas.

Pop Quiz #2

Approximately 50 percent of children in special education are identified as learning disabled. Of all children identified as learning disabled, _____ percent are primarily impaired in reading, and _____ percent of these reading impaired children have problems with the development of decoding.

      a. 20 percent; 10 percent

      b. 35 percent; 50 percent

      c. 80 percent; 90 percent

(Answer at the back of the book)

4
How Did We All Get This Way?

We are making tremendous progress in studying the neurobiology, but we don't yet have the definitive answers. Be skeptical. We have a long way to go.
Ken Pugh

Harvey,
What do you say?

I know I inherited my dyslexia. After my struggle in school and before I started this project, my father used to say that dyslexia was a crutch for me, and I was using it as an excuse. But as I became more involved in the dyslexia project, he began to learn with me. After he watched the first rough cut, he talked to me for the first time about his own troubles in school. Looking at me in the film, he saw himself. For the first time in my father's life, he had some insight into his own struggle. I had a new advocate, and soon, he became my biggest supporter, saying, "This movie must be made!" My dad was a pretty good speller and always liked to read, but he had his learning issues. This brings me back to what I said before – no two dyslexics are affected in the same way.

Scientists say that if you are dyslexic, there is a 40 percent chance that you will have a dyslexic child. My daughter is dyslexic, happy, doing well, and proud to be on the team. When I looked into it, I found other family members who didn't always do well in school. But they did do very well in the outside world. My grandfather was an inventor and CEO of the company named after his own father. He was a big-picture guy, a creative thinker, and I see in his example the combination of dyslexic strengths and weaknesses that scientists are currently researching.

Shayan Afshan
The Siena School, Silver Spring, Maryland

At Siena, I am having great experiences every day because I can learn something new and not struggle with it. I have trained for about a year and a half in Jiu JitsuI, and got my yellow belt after I got two first place medals at a competition.

Brain Specialists,

What do you say?

Gordon Sherman, PhD, Executive Director of Newgrange School and Education Center

The gene that has been identified as having a link to dyslexia has been linked in about 20 percent of cases, which is strong, but indicates that a lot of different genes are probably involved. There are a lot of ways to produce a brain with characteristics of dyslexia. You are never going to have any statement that applies to everybody. That's dyslexia.

One particular gene affects the way the cerebral cortex develops. The cerebral cortex plays a key role in higher cognitive function and in 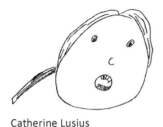 reading, writing, and spelling. We believe there is a great deal of variability in how the cerebral cortex is affected, but it probably happens during the gestational period. One of these genes affects neuronal migration, and if nature is manipulating that, you get differences in the way the brain is wired which influence processing and could produce something like dyslexia.

Catherine Lusius

Ken Pugh, PhD, President and Director of Research, Haskins Laboratories

The more I study dyslexia and the brain, and the more deeply I look at brain function and development, the more I'm convinced that there are real differences in how individuals can end up with this challenge. A challenge which almost always manifests in language, but might have different causalities in different individuals. That is why we need to understand the brain, so we can tailor our approach of remediation to an individual.

Guinevere Eden, PhD, Past President, International Dyslexia Association

Any parent who has dyslexia these days can be certain that his or her child has a 30 to 40 percent chance of also having dyslexia. A parent wants to be proactive in order to identify a child's dyslexia early, and then go ahead and start some of the interventions we know are effective, and tackle the problem before it becomes a big issue.

Gordon Sherman, PhD, Executive Director of Newgrange School and Education Center

There is variation in the brain in terms of the way that it looks and the way that it functions. We start out with a genetic program that gets us going at conception, but even in the uterus, there is a lot of environmental interaction with hormones, with nutrition, and sometimes with harmful things such as alcohol and drugs. And at birth, because the brain interacts with the environment, and no two environments are the same, these environments shape our brains differently, so by the time we are adults, we're all processing things differently. Our realities, our perceptions, and our consciousness are all different, so it is all about variation.

Mark Seidenberg, PhD, Senior Scientist, Haskins Laboratories

This is a strange moment in time. At this point, there are so many hypotheses about what might be going on with these children that you think they can't all be right. Everyone has his favorite theory, and we still haven't pinned down the underlying causes. I think it is going to turn out that dyslexia isn't just caused by one thing. Reading is a complicated system: it involves vision, speech, memory, reasoning, and learning. There are a lot of different ways a system like that could fail to develop normally. However, there may be certain kinds of deficits that tend to occur more often than others. We have to keep doing the research. We'll get to the bottom of it. Ten years, max. I truly think we are on the brink.

Richard Olson, PhD, Professor, Colorado Learning Disabilities Research Center

We are just starting to develop the field of molecular genetics related to reading difficulties, although we are well beyond where we began in the 1980s. In the mid-1980s, we were able to look at DNA and find that there was a region on the short arm of chromosome 6 that seemed to have a gene or genes related to the condition of dyslexia. In the past few years, there have been tremendous gains in the details we are able to see when we look at DNA. We have three billion base pairs that are the genetic code of genes, and that is a lot of base pairs to sift through and figure out. On average, all people differ by about one out of a thousand of those base pairs. We share our DNA almost completely, and from that perspective, we are all family. It doesn't matter what race we are or what region of the world we are from, we all have this very common pattern of DNA that essentially makes us human.

And then there are the one out of a thousand base pairs that differ in ways that give us curly or straight hair, light or dark skin, blue eyes, green eyes, and of course gender.

What I think has been hard for people to grasp is that there are also gene-related differences in how our brains work. From our own research, it is very clear that the huge proportion of the difficulty in learning to read in the population is related to genetic differences. Sometimes people draw the mistaken conclusion that if there is a genetic difference, it must mean that you can't do anything about it, but these genetic differences do not make it impossible to learn to read. For example, you can influence genetic disorders like diabetes by taking insulin. If you have nearsightedness, put your glasses on, and you will be fine, so the idea that a genetic disorder can sentence you to a state of slow learning in the area of reading is not true. In the population we are studying, about 60 percent of people have a reading difficulty that is influenced by their genes. That is a difficult concept because we want to think of people as having dyslexia for one particular reason, but often there is a real mix of reasons between genes and environment. If you push hard enough on the environment, you can get around those limitations to a large extent, and in almost all cases, become a functional reader. For kids with dyslexia, it is going to take a whole lot more work than it takes for typical kids to read.

Ken Pugh, PhD, President and Director of Research, Haskins Laboratories

I understand

We are making tremendous progress in studying the neurobiology, but we don't yet have the definitive answers. Be skeptical. We have a long way to go.

Nicky Harold

Stewart Mancano
Riverside School, Richmond, Virginia

At my old school I had to be taken away from my friends for several hours a day. It was difficult because they would rush you in classes. At Riverside, I felt great when I passed LFTS. It is a very hard test, and covers r-controlled syllables. It helps with writing, spelling and reading. I am also a champion gymnast, and my accomplishments include being State Champion, Boys Level 5.

5
How Is Dyslexia Diagnosed?

An assessment is not an end in itself, and it does not define the child, but a profile does allow us to build an educational program based on what the child needs.

Joyce Pickering

Harvey,
What do you say?

I grew up in Connecticut, only forty minutes away from Yale University, in New Haven, where my mother took me to be tested when she became alarmed at my lack of progress in school. I was in third grade. After a battery of tests (love that phrase), I went home with a diagnosis of dyslexia. Nice, but it meant nothing because no one knew what to do with that information.

Today's future dyslexics still experience a battery of tests, but it is a rousing, rock-flinging catapult compared to the wimpy, gentle little battery of my day, which I believe consisted mainly of the Woodcock-Johnson test. The experts I have been talking with tell me about handwriting samples, speech patterns, tests of phonological processing, a picture vocabulary test, tests of executive functioning, tests of visual motor functioning, and on and on and on. They use research-based measures to narrow down issues and zoom in on strengths and weaknesses.

Brain Specialists,

What do you say?

Guinevere Eden, PhD, Past President, International Dyslexia Association

Clinicians did a lot of the initial writing about people with dyslexia. Samuel Orton, an American neuropathologist, wrote about dyslexia and thought about it from the medical perspective. Macdonald Critchley, his counterpart in the United Kingdom, studied and wrote about dyslexic children from a neurological perspective. Critchley looked at their fine motor skills, their gross motor skills, and their reading skills. But keep in mind: they didn't have good measures of reading. They probably would have set children down, pulled up something that happened to be on the desk, and simply asked the children to read it. This is different from the kind of evaluation where we look at measures that are standardized and tightly correlated to predicting children's reading achievement.

Sylvia O. Richardson, MD, Past President, Orton Dyslexia Society

One of the major signs of risk in a young child is the slow acquisition of spoken language. They don't have phonemic awareness, and miss the rhymes in nursery rhymes. They may get confused with even two-part directions, and as a result, appear not to have listened to instructions when they really have. Children with dyslexia can also be clumsy. Fine motor tasks can be difficult: manipulating scissors and crayons, snapping, zipping, tying bows. These are markers to look for.

Gordon Sherman, PhD, Executive Director of Newgrange School and Education Center

To determine if someone has dyslexia, if we assess phonemic awareness, phonological processing, writing, spelling, reading comprehension, and fluency, we can get a pretty good idea.

Warning signs to look for are some difficulty with spoken language, difficulty pronouncing words, difficulty spelling simple words, and an inability to play with language, to manipulate language. Dyslexia has a genetic basis, so has anyone else in the family been diagnosed with it?

These days, it is not unusual for a father to be finally diagnosed with dyslexia when his son or daughter is diagnosed in school. Then he realizes that all those struggles he had in school weren't because he was misbehaving or stupid, but instead, he actually had a learning difference.

Guinevere Eden, PhD, Past President, International Dyslexia Association

It is important to have an evaluation that will allow people to understand your landscape of skills and where you have weaknesses and strengths. Understanding that you have dyslexia does help, because it explains why you have these difficulties, but more important is understanding the nitty-gritty detail of your strengths and weaknesses so that any intervention can map directly on some of the areas where you need help, and also take advantage of the areas where you have strengths.

Roger Saunders, Past President, International Dyslexia Association and helped found Jemicy School

Often the first clues for young children are that they get their *b's* and *d's* mixed up, or the *p's* and *q's*, or sometimes the *m's* are upside down and confused with *w's*. Teachers may notice those symptoms first, but there are earlier symptoms that are important too, in early language development. Sometimes children who seem very bright when they are three or four years old get frustrated when they can't find the words to express their thoughts and may stutter or mix up words.

Dee Rosenberg, Director of Education at Newgrange School

Domonic Cooper

Cognitive efficiency is an area in testing that involves tasks that must be done quickly and accurately. In many schools, you need to be very quick, especially in a classroom with a lot of students. If a teacher asks you a question, you need to answer in a hurry. In reading activities at school, you have to look at all those letters in a hurry and quickly come up with a word, and then read a whole sentence, and then a few more sentences, and keep it all in your mind, or it will affect your comprehension.

This also comes up in math. A teacher will give directions on how to do a math problem and then say, "Open up your textbooks to page thirty-seven and do one through nine," and if you haven't gotten that, it looks like you are not paying attention. But actually, you may be a person who needs more time for processing both the math explanation and the assignment directions.

Walker Meers
The Gow School, South Wales, New York

Gow has provided the help that I need, and the teachers here have an understanding. Before I came here, my teachers couldn't understand why I had trouble reading. They thought I was lazy. But

I'm not. I was a junior captain on our squash team in the 8th grade, and have done well in squash tournaments.

Teachers,
What do you say?

Joyce Pickering, SLC/CCC, CALT, QI, Hum D, Executive Director Emeritus of Shelton School

Sometimes preschoolers, three, four, or five years old, are referred to The Shelton School by their parents, by pediatricians, by occupational therapists, or by speech and language pathologists. These children usually have difficulty in one or more of four areas: coordination, language, attention, and perception, or CLAP for short. An assessment of motor skills reveals differences - sometimes subtle, sometimes more than subtle - in the development of gross or large motor skills and in fine motor skills such as the coordination of the hand.

Red flags wave if a speech and language assessment indicates possible difficulties with reading, writing, and spelling. Articulation difficulties beyond one or two sounds, when many words are unintelligible to most people, may indicate auditory processing deficits (where the child is not receiving sounds the way most children are) and continues to have errors like *wed* for *red* (when others have started to self-correct).

In the language area, we see children with a smaller vocabulary and more difficulty using words to express themselves. Although a parent might tell us a child chatters all the time, when we ask specific questions about the names for things, what you do with them, and how to describe them, we can see gaps in language development.

Nancy Xun Mi

While attention for a three-year-old is not what it is for an eight-year-old, there are average limits. Many of the children we work with have language difficulties, attention difficulties, and perceptual difficulties, and there is no way for most parents or preschool teachers who aren't trained to a high degree to know whether perception is developing normally or not. If we see a pattern in the testing that indicates weakness in those basic developmental areas, we will say only this: *This child is at risk for a learning difference because right now, skills are not where they would be in most children at that age.*

After forty-five years of teaching, I truly believe that most children want to succeed. They want to learn, and they don't want to punish themselves and suffer by not doing well. They want to see a happy look on their teacher's face and get stickers and make their parents proud. The impact is early and huge if children can't do the things they see others do. So if we see bright children who aren't succeeding, it is usually not because they aren't trying.

Nancy Cushen White, EdD, Associate Clinical Professor and Learning Disabilities Specialist

Often children are not identified with dyslexia until they start school. A student may have very good language comprehension and a good vocabulary. She may speak very well, and there may be no worries whatsoever that this child might have trouble in school. Then school starts, and this excited, motivated student begins to get stomachaches. I have heard this story over and over, so many times.

Arlene Sonday, Founding Fellow and first President of the Academy of Orton

Some parents will take their children for an outside evaluation, but it is expensive and many are priced out of that market. There are a number of states that will not accept dyslexia as a reasonable diagnosis. They don't believe in it, or they don't know how to deal with it.

Joyce Pickering, SLC/CCC, CALT, QI, Hum D, Executive Director Emeritus of Shelton School

To diagnose dyslexia, we use an educational battery, or group of tests, that incorporates measures of general intellectual functioning, processing ability, auditory and visual perceptual skills, academic skills, and attention skills. When we look at all of these tests, we don't focus on any one score, but on a profile of the child. Usually we see a normal or better mental ability score in children with dyslexia, who are usually better at communicating verbally.

Their greater difficulty is in putting their thoughts down on paper, and the auditory and visual processing scores are lower than for the average child with that mental ability. The academic scores are what we call *spotty*. So here is an intellect that's intact, and here is processing that's inaccurate and slower. And here is the impact of those processing deficits: difficulties in decoding - breaking words apart, sounding them out accurately; difficulties in encoding - hearing the sounds in a word and writing the word accurately; and difficulties in written expression - formulating thoughts and holding on to them while transferring them to paper using the code of language.

An assessment is not an end in itself, and it does not define the child, but a profile does allow us to build an educational program based on what that child needs.

Dyslexia Advocates,

What do you say?

Marcia Henry, PhD, Past President, International Dyslexia Association

An early sign for children who might be heading for trouble is a problem understanding the alphabetic system, and the fact that letters have corresponding sounds. Some children do not understand rhyme or have phonological awareness. These are all things that are difficult for children with dyslexia, and they are early signs for intervention.

Meg Bennett
The Hillside School, Macungie, Pennsylvania

In second grade at my old school, I confused nickels and dimes on a test. My teacher said I knew the answer and yelled at me. So I cheated. Here is what my parents say about me: Meg exudes creativity. It shines in every aspect of her life. Her independent spirit, bright perceptive nature and positive nature are engaging. She is a master multi-tasker with unlimited potential.

6
What Is School Like for Dyslexics?

Humiliation really affects your life when you're a kid. You accept that you're no good at this.
Billy Bob Thornton

Harvey,
What do you say?

Nicky Harold

I know now that I should've been working intensely on phonological awareness to catch up in grades two, three, four, and five, but that never happened, and by sixth grade, the idea was that if only they could get my coordination problem under control, that would solve all my problems in school. Did I mention that I also have dyspraxia? My fourth *dys*. This is better known in England than it is here. There, it is called *clumsy child syndrome*.

Those spelling bees were brutal in third and fourth grade. My spelling was atrocious. You could tell me all the basic rules, and I'd forget them before you stopped speaking. To this day, I still don't know *a* before *b* except after *c*. I mean, what are you talking about? It doesn't make sense to me. And when not much makes sense, you only have a couple of places to go. You could be the class clown. What are you going to do when you can't tie your shoes in the fourth grade because you don't know your left hand from your right hand? You know everyone's laughing at you because you're a joke. You may have a secret feeling that you're really not an idiot, but there are so many things that other kids can do just fine, and you can't do at all. The only refuge is to act like you're making them laugh on purpose. Maybe that's why Jay Leno became Jay Leno.

Or you could become dysfunctionally angry and bitter. That could be why our prisons are loaded with people who have learning differences. That could be why Lee Harvey Oswald became Lee Harvey Oswald, for all we know.

I grew up on a farm. I know what to do on a farm because I watched how something was done, and then I tried it myself. I learned by seeing and doing, with lots of movement and action. It wasn't easy for me to sit at a desk in school. Scientists have begun to figure this stuff out. Now they know to give the kid a trampoline to go bounce around on, or let him go off and run around so he can come back in and absorb information better.

In my day, students didn't sit together in little groups on carpeted floors and discuss perimeter or whatever. We had to sit at our desks in straight lines, and we had to be quiet. One of my teachers wrote, *Harvey doesn't work well in group situations. Harvey works best in one-on-one situations.* One-on-one meant my desk would be all by itself, pushed up against the teacher's desk on a really bad day. But usually, they left me in the big group, and it allowed me to drift into the back of the class near a window so I could gaze out and daydream.

My worst moment didn't come until I was in college, though. I actually took some college courses. On the second day of a writing class, the teacher held up a paper and asked, "Whose is this?" From our seats, we could all see how sloppy it was. Mine. The teacher went on and on about unacceptable work. He said, "By the time you get to my class, you are expected to know such and such." Then he told me to leave, out loud, in front of the entire class. I didn't feel like going back to any more writing classes after that. I felt like I was a bloody lost cause.

That was the last straw after so many other bad experiences in school. In high school, I wrote a book report on the *Planet of the Apes*. The teacher accused me of copying it off the back of my book. I didn't. I really had written it on my own, I really had understood the story, distilled it, and spit it back out, but she didn't believe I was capable of that. Later, I ended up winning an Emmy for writing. But a teacher couldn't believe I could do something well, and that really took the wind out of my sails for a while.

Brain Specialists,

What do you say?

Sylvia O. Richardson, MD, Past President, Orton Dyslexia Society

Melissa-Richter

Lots of these kids are distractible. They feel anxious about the fact that they can't do what's being asked of them. I've often thought that if someone gave me a job to do that I hated, that I didn't know anything about, and that I didn't know how to do, I'd be pretty darn angry, and I'd start squirming and moving around, and I'd try to get out of the bloody room. I'd want to crawl out the window, or do anything necessary to get out of there. Here you've got a kid who is just antsy, but he is a moving target for that teacher.

The difference between the child and the adult is that I could leave the job. I could get out, but he can't. He has to come every day and go through the same misery, and when he says, in so many words, "I want out of here," he gets in a lot of trouble.

Gordon Sherman, PhD, Executive Director of Newgrange School and Education Center

The learning challenges for a student with dyslexia aren't really apparent until about third grade. A child may have been doing fine in pre-K and kindergarten, but in the second half of kindergarten, more language instruction takes place. And right then, the child starts to feel a little different. The other kids seem to be catching on more. In first and second grades, differences become more obvious. There may be some language-related issues at this point, but many times, a child with a good visual memory can memorize words. Then in third grade, *BANG*, he hits the wall. There are so many new words that memory alone can't handle them. This may be a smart kid, a together kid, he can process information, he has friends, but he starts to wonder, *What's going on here?* Once reading to learn begins, the child with dyslexia falls behind very quickly. Self-esteem plummets, and as years go by, that self-esteem issue can turn into a lot of negative behavior.

However, on the athletic field, in music class, in interpersonal relationships, the child might be doing fine. This points out the importance of a multidimensional approach to life outside the classroom, so children can see clearly that they can do some things really well.

Roger Saunders, Past President, International Dyslexia Association and helped found Jemicy School

It depends upon the talent of the teacher to observe and understand the behaviors of children regarding language learning. Often children do misbehave because they're frustrated or embarrassed or scared that they are going to be asked to read out loud, or maybe they have gotten some *b's* backward and got laughed at. Teachers need to observe these details as part of the child's language learning difficulties rather than just as an emotional issue.

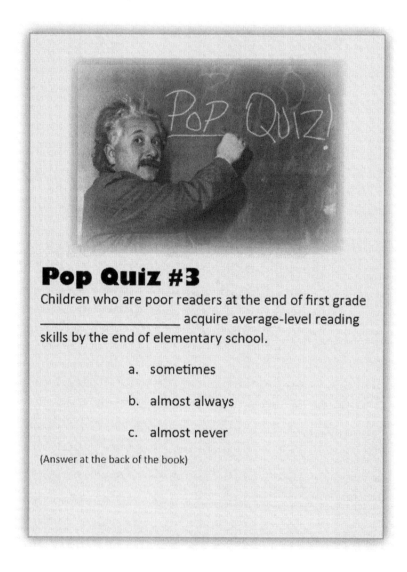

Pop Quiz #3

Children who are poor readers at the end of first grade
_____ acquire average-level reading
skills by the end of elementary school.

        a. sometimes

        b. almost always

        c. almost never

(Answer at the back of the book)

Sylvia O. Richardson, MD, Past President, Orton Dyslexia Society

To me, the teacher-training issue is the most serious problem that our children with dyslexia face because, for the most part, schools do not provide what they need. People may blame teachers, but that is wrong since they so often have never had the chance to learn how to teach these children.

Gordon Sherman, PhD, Executive Director of Newgrange School and Education Center

The real world is less time-dependent than a school is. Because something takes you five minutes longer, an hour longer, a day longer, or a week longer, if it is of equal or better quality, who cares? Being a slow processor in school makes your life very difficult, but in the real world it is not such an issue because you can select a field that meshes well with your processing characteristics.

Steve Frost, PhD, Senior Scientist, Haskins Laboratories

I had a hard time believing this, but now I have seen that some teachers really come poorly equipped to teach reading because there's such a pervasive attitude that reading is just something that children should be capable of learning. And if it is something children can't learn, then they are not smart.

Margie Gillis and her group bring teachers two things: great lessons on how to teach children and an understanding of what the problem is and what it isn't, that it isn't a problem with intelligence. It changes the attitude of many teachers to realize that reading is not like speech. As we have heard many times here at the lab, reading is difficult because speech is easy. We just pick up natural language naturally, and it is not the same with reading.

Ky Nicyper-Meryman
The Kildonan School, Amenia, New York

I hated my third grade teacher because she was very mean. She didn't like little kids. She put me out in the hall. I don't remember why she did this but it hurt my feelings. At Kildonan, when a lower school student got to be headmaster of the day, we did a slip and slide and got to make our own sundaes and ride on horses. My parents describe me as an energetic kid who never stops moving, so gymnastics is a natural fit for me. I have placed third on the bars at every New York state championship I have entered.

Sylvia O. Richardson, MD, Past President, Orton Dyslexia Society

Speech and language specialists have licensure and full accreditation and have had a different kind of training: clinical, not educational. They are exposed to neurology and scientific training that the educators do not get unless they are lucky. These speech and language specialists could help the classroom teacher understand more about language problems that some kids have, but what happens instead? The children go to the speech and language pathologist for a certain number minutes a day, and then they return to their classroom where they have missed part of the day's instruction. The classroom teacher doesn't know what the speech and language pathologist is working on and vice versa. It doesn't make sense, and the child is caught in the middle.

Gordon Sherman, PhD, Executive Director of Newgrange School and Education Center

If you are good in everything, with an A in social studies, and in math, and in English, and in science, you are considered a good student. Well, what happens if you're an off the charts, A+ terrific math student, and you're not doing so well in English, or social studies, or science? Now, are you an unsuccessful student, or an extremely successful student who is a specialist? In schools, we don't design well for specialists, but the real world is all about specialization.

And you are not a compensation. You are what you do in life, and what you do in life should be what your brain is good at, what you do really well, not just some compensation because your opportunities were so limited.

Sylvia O. Richardson, MD, Past President, Orton Dyslexia Society

Self-esteem is the result of success, and these youngsters must experience success in order to have any self-esteem. Many parents and teachers seem to feel that self-esteem can just be planted on a child: "Good job! Darling, you're such a fine young person, I just love you so much, and you are so wonderful." And the kid is thinking, *What's she talking about? I know I'm rotten. I can't read. I can't do it, and kids tease me all the time. Why is she saying this?* The adults think they are building self-esteem.

Gordon Sherman, PhD, Executive Director of Newgrange School and Education Center

Schools have got to learn that children not only need phonological processing, but also sensory motor development, motor development, and lots of repetition and practice. We don't give our children in school enough practice time. We expect them to read something now, and repeat it correctly tomorrow. This is ridiculous. Even adults don't do that well, but we ask it of children. Sometimes it takes years of daily practice for people to become fluent musicians or tennis players, and some children need that time to become fluent readers.

When a new technology develops, like the printing press or the computer, there are going to be some people who aren't naturally inclined to use it. They aren't necessarily disabled, but are wired differently, and need a plan for their education that is somewhat independent of the technology to which they are poorly suited. We must understand such cerebrodiversity and accept that there are a lot of different kinds of brains in our species. Cerebrodiversity results in learning differences, and while this is a good thing, we need to be clever to maximize the results. And as a society, we're not particularly clever at this. We're getting better, but we have a long way to go.

The environment can translate learning abilities into severe learning disabilities. We know that poorly designed instructional environments really punish cerebrodiversity. But the opposite is true, too. If the environment doesn't want what you don't have, it's not a disability.

Dyslexics,
What do you say?

***Colin Poole**,* Painter and sculptor

School was a b#@!%. It was like crawling over broken glass on your hands and knees. It was uncomfortable from start to finish. As I got into high school and then got into college, I came up with more coping mechanisms for figuring it out and how to work around things I couldn't do. But in grade school, it was very challenging because I was just not up to snuff with the average kids.

Malakai Graham
The Springer School and Center, Cincinnati, Ohio

At my old school, I fell behind a lot. I couldn't always get the help I needed. I felt sad when I had to miss some recess to finish my work. I have done better at Springer because my class has two teachers and they understand me. They have taught me strategies and they know how to help me learn better. I'm very good at drawing. I make my own comic books characters or I draw characters such as Huckleberry Finn or Tom Sawyer. I have my own website.

Charlie Phillips, Artist

I never understood math, and teachers kept saying, "Why don't you get this? What's wrong?" And I'd say, "You know, there is something wrong. I don't get it. Can you teach it another way?" And they'd say, "This is the only way. There's nothing else, that's it. If you don't get it, tough. You have to learn it this way. There is no other way, and there is nothing else we can do." That was a constant struggle for me. It was horrible, trying to figure out what was wrong, and trying to figure out what to do on my own.

Stephen J. Cannell, Writer, Producer

I went to school in the 1950s, and in my experience, no one recognized a condition called dyslexia. I am very verbal, so people could listen to my thinking when I was talking and realize, *This guy's got a good head on his shoulders.* So what I got all the time was, "You're not applying yourself. If you would just apply yourself, you would do so much better." Well, I would spend five hours studying for a test and tank it, and talk to a buddy who spent thirty minutes on it and got an A. After that scenario repeated itself half a dozen times, I started to say, *You know what? There's only one answer I have for all of this, and that is that he is a lot smarter than I am.* I was never told by students, or certainly not by my parents, that I was stupid. Nobody ever said that to me. I said that to me. I put that label on myself.

In high school, I had to write about a current event. I wrote a poem on Martin Luther King, Jr.'s attempt to desegregate schools in the South. I handed it in, about seven verses, and I got a B minus. I can still remember my grade because I didn't get B minuses; I got D's and F's. This was huge. I read it to my sister, two years ahead of me at a private school. I read it to my mom. I stood up at the dinner table, and I read it to all of them. The next morning at breakfast, I said I wanted to read my Martin Luther King, Jr. poem again, and my dad finally said,

"Okay we've heard your poem, Steve. That's enough," but that was a big moment for me: a B minus!

My sister came to me about a month later and said she had to write a poem for senior English and could she use mine? I reminded her that it was only a B minus poem, but she liked it, and she was my big sister, so I gave it to her. She copied it over in her handwriting, handed it in, and got an A. Her school published it in its literary magazine under her name. That was my first publication.

What does this tell us? *Perception drives result.* I got a B minus because my instructor knew I was no good and felt he was cutting me a lot of slack. Even when they are doing A-quality work, some kids are getting B minuses and C's because their teacher thinks, *This isn't that good.* It is all based on perception.

Stephanie Elgendi
Morning Star School, Tampa, Florida

The kids at my old school used to laugh at me because I couldn't read or spell. They also said I wasn't dyslexic when I really was. They said I had no hope and wanted to put me with mentally handicapped kids. At Morning Star,  the teachers make learning fun. They tell me I have special gifts for memorizing songs and lines, and singing on pitch. I was the star in the school Christmas play and Gala!

Sarah Joy Brown, Emmy Award-winning actress

It seems that with dyslexia, everything is good and fine until you're five, and then suddenly you're in school and you're a dummy. You may have been very intuitive and really good at certain things like sports, but suddenly, it all goes wrong. I feel like I missed a lot because I didn't learn the way the teachers taught. I needed something visual to look at. I needed to be able to listen to stories. I didn't read a book until I was in the twelfth grade, but I still maintained A's and B's because I could memorize everything. So if a friend would read me her book report, I could memorize it well enough to get an A on the test. I found a way to compensate, and I think many dyslexics are successful when they learn to compensate for the way that their brains work.

Kendrick Meek, Former member of U.S. House of Representatives from Florida's 17th District

My first few years of school were typical. At that time there wasn't really any great focus on disabilities or who was ahead or behind. Pretty much all kids were equal. It wasn't until third grade that there was some recognition that something was different with me. We started addition, and my teacher said, "Something is not happening with Kendrick. He's not keeping up with the rest of the class. He's not interested in what we are talking about, but he seems to be a normal kid." I began fooling around, falling behind in class, and they moved me into a class with kids with physical handicaps. I did learn sign language through that experience.

By third or fourth grade, they diagnosed me with dyslexia. I repeated fifth grade, and by sixth grade my mother went to the school and said, "It might be very detrimental to Kendrick's development if you hold him back again." So they decided that I should go to junior high school and stay with my original class.

My mom held her ground because she thought that I had just as much smarts as the next kid, and I deserved to move on. I attribute a lot of my later success to my mother, an educator who understood child development. She learned about learning disabilities and dyslexia, and then taught me about them; I will be forever indebted to her for that. I could have been that big kid, just falling farther and farther behind.

Kyle Morrissey, Graduate of The Kildonan School

When I got to kindergarten, school wasn't so great, and when I was six, it was rough. In second grade, I got to the point where I was tested for dyslexia – I was told, "Oh, you don't have it." Even back then, I was really good in history. That's the subject that I took comfort in. I never thought I was stupid. I just thought I wasn't good at reading or writing. In fourth grade, I was finally tested by someone outside of the school, and I found out that I do have dyslexia. But even then, they didn't do much for me. I did horribly in math. I only like math when it applies to something.

My knowledge of history grew and grew. I learned about history when my grandma and my parents read books to me. I couldn't read, but I looked at the pictures. And I would read the words I could, and skip the rest. The idea of the past intrigued me. I used to go to reenactments when I was young so I could imagine the scenes.

Daniel Cortez, Graduate of The Kildonan School

Before I knew I was dyslexic, I just knew I couldn't read stuff that other kids could. When I was at public school, I got confused with words. When I saw words, I would think, *What is this stuff? What is it saying?* I used to always try, but the sounds never got to me. I used to copy down what it said in the dictionary, but I never knew what it meant. I never knew what the definition was. People made fun of me.

I remember when I was in fifth grade they used to call me retarded because I was in the slower classes. I couldn't spell words. They never helped me out much. It was like, if you don't know it, you don't know it. And I got a bad grade. They didn't really care. It made me feel like no one was helping me.

When I got to The Kildonan School, I started to learn, and I started to feel smart in my head. Diana King started teaching me what the sounds mean. I can break down the words. I can read a lot better now.

Dyslexia is both a learning disability and a teaching disability. It has to do with how you learn and how they teach. A little bit of both.

When I grow up, I want to be the person that draws how to build houses. I want to be an architect.

Joe Pantoliano, Emmy Award-winning actor

By the time I hit the tenth grade, the schools had it set up so I was in the worst group of kids. We were kids who either had some kind of autism or retardation. At Cliffside Park High School, there was the top academic group, the general education group, the woodshop/workshop guys who would go off and work with cars, and then there was my group. I would just move from one classroom to the next, sleeping on my desk. That was okay as long as we didn't make a sound, and as long as we didn't start any trouble or light any cherry bombs off in the toilet. We had Doc Banarsi, a doctor of mathematics. He also taught math at St. Peter's in Jersey City. His day job with us was more like being a policeman. As long as we didn't cause any problems, we got passed through. By the fifth grade, they started just passing me through; before that, I remember getting left back.

I had just turned five when I started school. I went for six months, and I got left back. I graduated kindergarten, and then in the first grade, I was held back into 1A. And then, I was left back again in the second grade, and then in the third grade they eliminated the A and B scenario, so it was a full year, and I got skipped ahead. By the time I got to the fourth grade, I was thoroughly confused. I was probably a year and a half behind at that time, in the fourth grade with a second-grade reading level.

My teacher was so frustrated, it was horrible. I think her frustration was justified, but her behavior wasn't. She made an example of us one day because of our inability, or in her mind, unwillingness to learn. She said that the three of us weren't entitled to read, and she took our books away in a huff. Maybe she gave us our books back the next day, but the point was made, and the stigma was set. And from that point on, I shut down. I didn't give a shit.

Cary Spier, Parent of Sarah Spier, dyslexic, and documentary filmmaker

When I was young, I was really good at sports and the theater. As soon as I figured that out, I just stuck to them. But the classroom was disastrous. I really felt like an idiot. But I could run the fastest, throw a ball the farthest, and really smack that volleyball, so I tried to stick to the things I felt good about. I knew that school was not going to be my specialty, and I tried to get through it as quickly as possible and never look back. I went to USC film school, and I went right to work in Hollywood. I've been working in the film industry ever since.

Sarah Joy Brown, Emmy Award-winning actress

I was ranked in the top eight percent of students in mathematics when I was in second grade, and I think my worst moment in school came the next year in third grade when I suddenly began to really, really struggle with it. Math just got too big. I struggled with concepts beyond simple multiplication and addition, and I remember being pulled out of class to sit with the kids I perceived had something wrong with them. I remember thinking to myself, *Wow, what happened? I guess now I'm stupid.*

Fortunately, I had other things in my life that I was good at, so it didn't affect my self-esteem too much, but it was a big deal to my father. He couldn't understand why I couldn't do math anymore. In his way of thinking, you are supposed to be good at math and reading in the way that it's typically taught. He certainly wouldn't have appreciated anybody saying that I was learning disabled, but I was. If someone had pointed out, *She has a learning difference and needs to be taught in a different way,* I probably would have gone further mathematically than I was ever able to go. But I couldn't communicate to my teachers that I learned differently. I would ask, "Why is two plus two four? Why?" They said, "It just is. That's the way it is." At that point the dyslexic brain can shut down.

Joe Pantoliano, Emmy Award-winning actor

Each year, during the first several days of school, I would come to my new classroom and sit right in front of the teacher in the first row because I knew that she was going to ask us all to read out loud. I'd think, *Let's get this shit over with,* and I would read once and that would be the last time she would ever call on me. But we'd always have to go through that first, so she could size us up and figure out who's who.

Kyle Morrissey, Graduate of The Kildonan School

My worst moment ever in school was when I was in fifth grade. Towards the end of the year, there was this program where the fifth

graders were told to read to the first graders. The teachers knew I had a problem reading, but they told me to do it anyway. I took the book and walked off to a corner to read to the first grader, but I could not even read that simple book.

Jessie Warzybuk

Kim Bucciantini, Graduate of The Forman School

It was hard for me, especially when the teacher said I had to write an assignment. I wrote really big, and I couldn't write on the lines, so what should have been one page turned out to be two pages with scribbles all over. More than anything, it made me angry because the teacher knew I couldn't write. She knew. I think she must have thought the more she made me write things out by hand, the better my handwriting would get, but it just didn't happen. I tried to concentrate as hard as I could on it, but that just made my handwriting worse. Eventually, I was allowed to type in school.

Zach Capriotti, Inmate at State Correctional Institution

When I was in school, the teachers would send me to detention. One time they had me in the detention room for thirty days with no books, no nothing, just me in the room. And then they pulled me out of the room to take some test. I did very poorly on that test because your mind kind of slows down when you are closed up like that.

Joe Pantoliano, Emmy Award-winning actor

I got some help at Demarest. It's an alternative high school. Every once in a while, I found someone who would just sit me down and say,

"Look kid, you can do this." And at Demarest, I remember being able to take a test orally. I got a 95, and the whole class applauded me. The teacher said, "You see that, Joe?" That was a big deal. After that came a series of more disappointments.

I wouldn't do the work. I would be defiant. "Do you have your work?" No. "Why didn't you do it?" Didn't want to. The only reason I stayed in school was because if I left, I'd have to be around my mother more, and I'd have to get a job. I was working after school anyway. I just wanted to be able to get a diploma.

I cheated off the smartest kid in school on my SATs. I don't want to get the guy who helped me in trouble, but if you looked up Joe Pantoliano's SATs in 1970, you'll see really high scores. I never took algebra, I never took any kind of math because, forget about numbers, I still count with my fingers. That's the only way I can figure out a tip.

Olivia Hanson, Graduate of The Forman School

A student might be trying hard, but if teachers don't think she is and just keep bashing her, she is going to give up and not care. They've got to keep encouraging her. If a student is struggling, they've got to spend the time, even if it takes forever, to break the lesson down until she understands. It is difficult for her, so they should be as nice as they can, and not put her down because that hurts more than they think. And that's not a good feeling to keep going to school with every day.

Kendrick Meek, Former member of U.S. House of Representatives from Florida's 17th District

In high school, I tried to hide the fact that I had dyslexia. I was in special education classes. But because I was a big jock and a captain on the football team, I was one of the school leaders. Everyone knew me. I was big number 99, an all-county player, a very popular athlete. I spent half my day in regular classes and half in the LD classes for the learning disabled. I remember that after the bell, I would always make it to class in two minutes. I would stand in the corner of the room as people walked down the hall so they wouldn't see that I was in the LD class. And then when the bell rang to start class, I would sit down, but not in view of the little window in the door where someone might see who was in there, because students made jokes about the kids in that class. Most students didn't know that I was in there.

Jack Horner, Paleontologist

I grew up in Shelby, Montana, up near the Canadian border. I liked digging holes in the ground, I liked getting dirty, and I wanted to be a paleontologist for as long as I can remember. When you want to be a paleontologist, when you want to be a discoverer and explorer, you learn that you don't walk around looking at the world; you walk around looking at the ground. And for children who have a problem in school, looking at the ground is a good thing. Like many who have dyslexia, I was thought to be lazy and stupid in school. I didn't feel good about myself. I went to college, but I flunked out seven times. I went to the University of Montana to be a paleontologist, but I failed all the classes I took, including paleontology.

Phil Marandola, Graduate of The Forman School

In elementary school, my teacher would keep me in from recess. I needed to get out and play and get my energy out, but I had to stay back in the classroom, practicing verbs and prepositions. It was difficult, but I definitely tried. Writing was the hardest for me. I had a hard time even sitting down to write, and then they threw cursive at me. It was like a whole different language.

Kayla Rider
Riverside School, Richmond, Virginia

In public school my worst experience was when we were doing two-digit multiplication but I didn't get it and was afraid to raise my hand. At Riverside, I really like when I get to go to Language Fundamentals. My LF teacher said that I was cheerful and eager to learn. I'm on a puppet team and we go churches, schools, charities and much more! I also get picked by my team to do most of the lead parts.

Aaron McLane, Special Effects Artist

I had a few good teachers who dealt with me well, but then there were the types who just pushed me through. They'd always pass me. I could draw very well, so they'd say, "Oh here, draw this picture for a project, and you can pass the class." I would draw their picture, and they'd be happy and pass me, but they wouldn't take the extra time to help me understand what they were teaching.

I had to leave my class twice a week and go to tutoring, and we would study phonics like roots, suffixes, and prefixes, and learn all that stuff so I wouldn't have trouble reading. And I did learn tricks about reading. We'd read books together and do math. But the funny thing was when I was doing badly at school, I'd go to the tutoring, but I'd be missing class, so it didn't help me at all. Things got worse.

I'm left-handed, so writing became really hard. I still can't write. People tell me they can't read my handwriting. Well, sorry. But I really like to read. I really got into reading, and I really got into drawing and artistic things. In first grade, my teacher took away my red crayon because I drew too many scary things. I wasn't allowed to draw scary things anymore. I had an overactive imagination, but I didn't do too well in the spelling area. Now I create special effects for movies.

Eric Steinberg, Parent and dyslexic

I used to feel absolute panic in school if I had to read out loud. If we were reading in a circle, I would figure out where my part would be and read it over and over and over, trying to figure out every word, so that when it came to my turn, I had it memorized. I would get increasingly nervous as the reading moved around the circle and got closer and closer to me. Could I get up and go to the bathroom, so they would finish before I got back? Would the bell ring? Could I somehow just disappear? Something, anything, so that I wouldn't have to read.

The place they gave us for remedial reading was where they kept all the balls to check out for recess. There were three or four of us with our remedial reading teacher in this sort of wide hallway with all the balls. We didn't even have a classroom to go to. I can look in my mind's eye and picture that place perfectly.

Billy Bob Thornton, Musician, Actor, and Filmmaker

I was actually berated by my algebra teacher, and so I thought I was dumb. I looked around at all the kids who made A's and B's in algebra and geometry and saw them as mythic figures. I thought, *These people can do algebra, where they give you the answer, and you're supposed to figure out the question. How do they do that? And they can add letters. How do you add an X to a Y?* Just adding regular numbers made my head hurt, let alone all this gibberish.

My teacher would send me to the board to work an algebra problem, and I would just stand there. It wasn't like being given five or six puzzle pieces, and you get part of the pig together but can't find which piece is the tail - I didn't even know what it was. It was like handing me a puzzle and just leaving the room. I didn't even have the concept of what I was supposed to do with this thing, so I would just stand there. Humiliation like that really affects your life when you're a kid. You accept that you're no good at this.

I would work harder at things I was interested in. Even though history was difficult to read, it had stories, it had wars, it was exciting. I was good at history, even though it was painful.

Phil Marandola, Graduate of The Forman School

I was a public school student from sixth to ninth grade. Instead of sending us to the library with all the other kids for a study hall, they stuck the kids with learning differences in a room with kids with autism, and told us to do homework there for an hour a day. We were in there with a football coach. He was trained to be a coach, but he didn't know how to help us. He was over there writing up plays while we were trying to learn algebra.

Teachers didn't know how to teach us. They'd see us trying to be like the other kids, but we'd still be failing. They didn't see how hard we were working.

Kendrick Meek, Former member of U.S. House of Representatives from Florida's 17ᵗʰ District

When I meet folks and they discover I have dyslexia, they often have low expectations of me. I look forward to not only proving them wrong but also to bringing about a shift in their mind about people with dyslexia. It means a lot when they realize that people who live around them, who entertain them, or who govern them, may have dyslexia. It wasn't until I learned that so many others around me had some kind of learning difference that I started talking openly about my dyslexia. Now I am fine with that.

After college, when I was attending the state highway patrol academy, I will never forget a test we had dealing with radar, full of mathematical questions. I failed the first test, and you can only fail two tests in the patrol academy before they send you on your way. I went to the first lieutenant and explained that I have dyslexia and sometimes I don't see numbers as I should. After I gave him my long story, he looked at me from behind his desk and said, "Son, I just want to let you know that the rules are the rules, and if you fail one more test, you are out of the academy." That was the first time in my life that I was really slapped with the reality that if you can't perform to the standard, no one cares that you have a disability or that it's hard for you to keep up with the rest of the class. I realized that in the real world there are no tutors, and there are no educators who understand your plight.

It was then that I started to apply myself even more. I thought I had been applying myself in college, and in high school, and in junior high school, and even elementary school. But I always had someone around who would go to bat for me. Now, my mother couldn't help me. No one could.

I studied constantly, and if things didn't make sense, I went over them again. After lights went out at ten o'clock, I would study by flashlight. After my flashlight burned out, I would go to the bathroom stall and sit and study until one in the morning. Then I would get up at five o'clock. I applied myself, I worked hard, and I prayed a lot. And I didn't fail the test. I graduated from the patrol academy and became a decorated trooper on the road. As the result of making a DUI arrest in 1991, I became the number one trooper in the state. I served on the governor's security detail, and that led me to the state legislature. The fact that I had to perform better than the next person was a good lesson for me, especially in public service.

Katie Kirkland
The Shelton School, Dallas, Texas

Once in reading class the teacher called on me and I couldn't read one word. The teacher said I could do it, but I really couldn't! Me! Not only did she ask me one time, but she continued to put me on the spot. At Shelton, I realized I was just like everyone else

at school. I wasn't the odd one out any more and I didn't have to hide or pray that the teacher wouldn't call on me. I am very artistic and am an accomplished equestrian. I have been ranked fourth in the nation and have ribboned at Worlds. I also create jewelry. My pieces are selling in high end boutiques, Neiman Marcus, and Saks Fifth Avenue.

Billy Blanks, Inventor of Tae Bo exercise program, fitness guru

I was the only one of my ten brothers who had a problem reading. I liked numbers and could do math, but it was very hard for me to be able to read something and comprehend it.

I used to hate going to school because I was the only one of my brothers who rode the yellow bus. I was ashamed and nervous that someone would see me on it and know that I was in special education. Kids always made fun of me. I would do my best to hide because I felt different, and didn't know how to deal with that.

I was labeled mentally handicapped and put in special classes. We played a lot of basketball, or maybe some football, or we'd go to the gym. Sometimes we'd have a little reading test, but most of the teachers didn't know what to do with us. They had all different types of kids in that room, so how were they going to help each one of us?

I liked physical fitness and wanted to get involved with martial arts because I saw that it really disciplined a person. I thought it would help me focus. We couldn't afford classes, so I had to wait until a youth center was built in our neighborhood. When I finally got involved in a karate program, it helped me with school because it gave me the power to see that even if I couldn't read I could become good at other things in my life.

My teachers couldn't see what I needed because they only saw me from the outside. But if they could have figured out what was going on inside me, maybe they could have given me a physical fitness program that would have helped me be a better reader. Maybe they could have found a fun way to teach me to spell. But people don't want to change, and they must have figured they would just teach everybody the same way.

My worst moment in school was when they told me I was mentally retarded. I felt, *Oh my God! Now I'm different from everyone else, and people are going to make fun of me.* I had to go home and tell my fifteen brothers and sisters, *I'm the different one, I'm the oddball of the family.* It was hard to let my father and mother down. People said there was something mentally wrong with me, and that was hard to take as a parent and as a kid. I had to watch my brothers become great athletes; I was the only one who couldn't because I was too shy and embarrassed to get in front of people and make any mistakes.

When I had to read out loud in class, I wouldn't do it. I was too embarrassed and too nervous. I just didn't feel confident enough to read in front of other kids because, even in special education, all they do is look at you and laugh. *You're stupid! You're retarded!* What I would do is act tough. "I ain't doing that. Send me to the principal, but I ain't doing it." Then I would have to face the consequences when I went home, and I would get disciplined because of what happened at school, but I would rather go through that then get up and embarrass myself in front of my friends. What's the point of being in special education if people just make fun of you? That was my compensation, acting tough.

Luke Bornheimer, Graduate of The Forman School

During my eighth grade year, I was diagnosed with decoding disabilities, which is breaking a word down, and encoding disabilities, which is putting a word back together and understanding its meaning. I also had trouble with organizational skills. But I was fine until the amount of reading really picked up. That's when it started to hurt a little more.

If no one knows that I am the only kid with learning issues in the room, then it feels like more of a learning *difference* because I can usually keep up with everyone else as long as it is a task I can do. But if people know about me and they discriminate, maybe not even blatantly, but just thinking about it, then it becomes more of a disability. I think it is not how the kids who are different act or feel or what they think about themselves, I think it is how others view them that takes it from a learning difference to a learning disability.

Cary Spier, Parent of Sarah Spier, dyslexic, and documentary filmmaker

The first time I was panic-stricken in a classroom was during one of those standardized tests in fifth grade. All the kids were zipping through, marking their little circles, and I didn't even read the questions after I realized I couldn't do the first five. I just drew a picture with my little dots, and my parents got called in. At that point, I knew something was wrong, but they didn't really talk about dyslexia when I was a child. I guess I just thought I was stupid. But because I was so panicked in school, I did learn to quickly think my way out of things. I'm a quick thinker on my toes. I think that dyslexics develop that.

So when Sarah had trouble in school, I immediately recognized what it was all about and I said, "I will never allow my child to feel stupid like I did." It was a fight all through her years in school, making her feel special, not stupid, not letting her think she had a disease, but a gift. Still, she was ridiculed, she was humiliated, and I would have to take her out of one school and put her in another. We worked together to get her through school.

Sarah Spier, Founder and President of Mwambao Alliance, Mwambao Primary School, Tanzania

I remember an English class in seventh grade where we had to read our papers in front of everybody. It was so hard for me, not just to read but to get up in front of an audience, especially when I was reading my own work and telling people what I was thinking. I got up, but I could not speak. In seventh grade, I got D's and F's, and I locked myself in the bathroom every lunch. I sat by myself, crying. I didn't understand why I was so different.

Jack Horner, Paleontologist

When I was a student, teachers frequently sent notes home saying that I was lazy. But in high school every year, I made a science project because there was no time limit on it. I could make something at my own speed, and I won all the science fairs that I entered, all four years. I was failing science, but getting the grand prize for the science fair. It's unclear how I graduated from high school. My English teacher gave me a D minus, minus, minus, and he said that meant that I failed English, but he didn't ever want to see me again. I sent him a copy of my first book, for spite.

Parents,
What do you say?

Olivia Card

Carol Hill, Parent and educational advocate for dyslexics

Many adults remember being the youngsters in those classes in the back of the stage or way off to the side of the building down a secluded hallway. They were the kids still in class while the rest of the school was out at recess. It was humiliating to feel obviously different and inadequate. We know now that warehousing children together with different learning and life challenges around the same table doesn't allow the particular recipe of success for dyslexic students. Teachers spend huge chunks of time correcting behaviors, getting each student started on different working levels, and dealing with multiple sets of materials. I've seen students with dyslexia, with average to above-average intelligence and no behavior problems, receiving no more than five minutes of focused attention in this type of class. Dyslexic students are not squeaky wheels. But they do need explicit instruction and multisensory practice to be successful in reading, writing, and spelling skills.

I have seen my children in situations that I knew hurt them. My son worked very hard all through fourth grade, and was excited to be able to read his own report card for the first time. He opened it before I could get to it, and the first line he read about himself was, *Callum needs to work a lot harder at handing in his papers and finishing his work. I'm disappointed in him.* He put the paper down, went up to his room, put his face to the wall, and wouldn't talk to me. This is unnecessary. This is ignorance. This is people thinking that my child has a character flaw, when he was probably working harder than any other child in that classroom. When an authority says such a thing, a child thinks, *Maybe it's true,* and remembers it for a long, long time. That's unacceptable for my child, your child, any child.

Diana Naples, New York branch of International Dyslexia Association

My daughter's elementary school used a whole language approach, but she was lucky enough to get the mature teachers who had been trained to teach phonics and still used phonics in the classroom. She benefited from that, and everything clicked together. My son's kindergarten teacher was fresh out of graduate school. I wanted to ask him, "What are you trained in? What are you doing?" I don't want a reading specialist. I don't want a special education teacher. I want a classroom teacher who is trained to use a multisensory approach.

I remember I thought my son was reading. I didn't realize that he actually wasn't reading because he had the books memorized. Quite often, he was on a different page than we were, but I just thought… well, heaven knows what I thought. By the end of fourth grade, we were in a bit of a mess.

Because my son wasn't reading, there was a lot of frustration and anger, and the resource room the school provided wasn't working. They had us put him in a Saturday morning program. He met one-on-one with a teacher every morning before school. He went to summer school. And out of my own pocket, I paid for a tutor, another first-grade teacher who said she had taught many first graders to read. But it wasn't working. Then I found the International Dyslexia Association, and through the IDA I found The Kildonan School. After six weeks of summer camp there, my son told us that he learned more than he had in his whole life. They used Orton-Gillingham methods, and that's what worked.

Carol Hill, Parent and educational advocate for dyslexics

Dyslexic children do not have an obvious, physical learning disability. Very, very often, the learning challenge remains obscure until the fourth or fifth grade. This is how we missed the cues with the first of our three dyslexic children. In fact, Siobhan herself was the one who came forward and said that she suspected something was not right, and asked, in fourth grade, to be tested. This was handled by our public school. At the formal meeting, the school psychologist said, "She is a square peg, and she has to learn how to live in a round hole. She is manipulative, and dramatic, and creative, and she's just manipulating you."

After much counseling, Siobhan finally said, "You know, I'm tired out by counselors telling me how to feel better about stuff after it's happened. I want it to stop happening! I need somebody to help me to have some control so I can just feel wanted and do well in school."

Voncille Wright, Parent of Jo'Von Wright

By the time Jo'Von was in the third grade, I knew something was really going wrong. Her teachers didn't see it because she was very articulate, friendly, and outgoing, and they weren't willing to agree with me that there could be some learning difficulties there. But in essence, she had already lost first and second grade.

In third grade, she began to feel quite isolated because she realized that she was not moving along with the other students, and started to exhibit some behaviors that we didn't like. She would shut down, she would appear uncooperative, she would appear to be sleepy and tired, anything she could do to get out of work because she couldn't do it, and she couldn't figure out why she couldn't do it.

We started pulling her out of the third grade classroom to go for some additional help. I asked for some testing, and they were a little bit slow getting that started, saying, "Well, she started school at four, so she is probably just lagging behind." It took a full year before I could convince the staff that we really needed to take a look at what was going on here. That's when we discovered that she did have a learning disability. They weren't able to tell me what kind of learning disability at that point, but they knew that there was something wrong.

They would almost hate to see me coming. I would walk in and see the eyes rolling, "Oh, here comes Mrs. Wright again!" It got to the point where I would take time off work to sit there at school so I could figure out what was going on. We hired a private tutor for

Jo'Von, and although she made some progress, it was very, very slow and very, very painful... not only for the tutor (ha ha), but also for Jo'Von. It would take us most of every evening to go over some simple homework. Because Jo'Von was feeling stressed, we were feeling stressed, and we still didn't have a handle on what the problem was.

As they pulled her for more time in the resource room, Jo'Von started missing out on the content areas in the fourth and fifth grade, and had little science or history, all very meaningful subjects that build on prior knowledge. And she still wasn't learning how to read. She was getting special help in the class, plus we hired a tutor, plus she was getting additional help at home, and it still wasn't working. Something wasn't right, and the school did not want to listen to me. It was her fifth grade teacher who suggested that I pull her from the school because they were just not able to help her. And that's sad because it's a public school. My bachelor's degree is in special education, and I was able to identify some issues, but I would have thought that someone with a more recent degree would have been able to provide more assistance. But they just couldn't do it.

Jo'Von became a very sad person. She started making all kinds of excuses because she didn't want to go to school. She was sick, she had a headache, she had a stomachache. I understood the pain outsiders couldn't see. They didn't know the Jo'Von in the kitchen, the Jo'Von in her bedroom, the Jo'Von who cried because she didn't want to go to school.

Jacob Garwood
Friendship School, Eldersburg, Maryland

The werst thing that hapend once was wen my techer got mad at me because I couldn't anser a math problem. The best thing at Friendship school is wen I lrned to rite a ecspanded paregraf. It felt so good to get my thots on paper.

Teachers,
What do you say?

Joyce Pickering, SLC/CCC, CALT, QI, Hum D, Executive Director Emeritus of Shelton School

Frequently, we see a child withdraw to a seat in the back of the classroom to avoid eye contact with the teacher, sending the clear message, *Don't call on me, don't embarrass me.* If the teacher does call on him, often the child will use the technique of covering his mouth and mumbling, so if he is wrong, maybe the teacher will think she didn't understand him. A lot of teachers are very sensitive and kind and don't want to embarrass this little person, so they stop calling on him. Nice, but it doesn't help him learn much.

Robin Winternitz, Dyslexia advocate and educational consultant

In the classroom environment, a lot of the ways that children who are dyslexic will mask their inability to read is to draw attention to themselves. That sounds strange, but that's what they'll do. They will make jokes and carry on until the class is riled up and the teacher is off task, and then they won't have to read out loud. Another thing kids do is rely on their peers. The literature in first, second, and third grade has a lot of visual cues, so if children are strong visually, they don't need to read all those words. They can listen to everybody else and look at the pictures, and everybody thinks they are reading. Other children get the school stomachache on days when they know they will have to read in front of others. Some develop a school phobia because they've been treated so poorly in the school environment; they just don't want to go anymore. The trauma that children go through is just amazing.

Joyce Pickering, SLC/CCC, CALT, QI, Hum D, Executive Director Emeritus of Shelton School

In the preschool years, many of these children are very aware of the difficulties they are having, but some develop ways to compensate and go through the first and second grades looking to many as if they are learning to read. My explanation for this is that many of them are very good guessers, they have a good vocabulary, and they can memorize quickly what they hear other people reading. They can look at pictures in the little books and tell the story, but they can't call the words accurately off the page. When I ask a teacher why he didn't help a student decode the text more accurately, I often hear what most teachers are trained to believe: that the end goal of reading is comprehension, and the child did get the parts of the story in. Well, the end goal of reading *is* comprehension, but if children continue to decode inaccurately, their comprehension will decrease.

Diana Hanbury King, Founder of The Kildonan School

As I read through your elementary records, Harvey, I see that someone wrote, *Phonics ability is very poor.* I have to ask, if your phonics ability was very poor, why wasn't it remediated? With training, that can improve. You are described as a likeable boy, and that is typical with dyslexic students whose keen powers of observation nearly always lead to innate charm. So I would expect that. These are cute kids, and nearly all of them are innately charming. And because teachers tend to like them, they tend not to fail them, so they keep these students going and keep pushing them on and on.

Eventually the students find themselves in a situation with expectations that they can't possibly meet. So they either continue to be sweet and charming, or find other ways to occupy themselves by disrupting the class or tuning out. All of this is typical, and the usual response is to blame a child's speech problem, or blame a lack of maturity, or blame this, that, and the other.

Robin Winternitz, Dyslexia advocate and educational consultant

The class clown finds another way to get attention, since he can't get any attention for doing good work. And there is the aggressive one, who is always acting out. These children are just so angry. They know they are as smart as the other kids, but they also know they can't do the same things, and they have no idea why. Many of the children who come to us from other schools are quite wounded. No matter what they achieve, some can't ever put that pain behind them. I've seen successful adults, extremely confident people who run businesses, break down and start crying when the subject turns to writing on the blackboard in third grade. Those are serious wounds, and I think we need to do everything we can to stop inflicting them.

Most parents know if their child is a little different. Once they see that, they go to the public school system and say, "Okay, what's going on here? My child isn't learning like his older brother or sister or the kid next door did. Help me." And a lot of times the school system will say, "Well, your child didn't fall below this level after we did the testing." If he is not far enough below grade level, the school will say, "Oh, he'll outgrow that. It will be fine. We'll throw a little tutoring here, or you can go get some outside tutoring, and that'll be fine. Maybe you need speech and language services or occupational therapy. Everything will be fine."

What happens is that the child hits fourth or fifth grade, and if he has learning problems of any kind, that's where he falls to pieces. The parents go back to the school and say, "Okay, now my kid's failing. What am I supposed to do?" That's where the money comes in again, and people will go to private assessments and private tutoring. And if they've just gone to an average tutor who does academic tutoring, that's not going to help the child.

Jorge Miranda
The Hillside School, Macungie, Pennsylvania

Once a teacher told me to hurry up you slow kid when I was trying to write. I am happy to be at the Hillside School where I am improving my reading. I also like that kids don't make fun of me. I have been on a swim team since third grade, and have won many medals and ribbons, including a silver championship in New Jersey.

Nancy Cushen White, EdD, Associate Clinical Professor and Learning Disabilities Specialist

We know that everyone learns differently. And there certainly are techniques that benefit all students and hurt none. On the other hand, there are some students who can't survive without certain kinds of teaching techniques. What worries me is if everybody gets a little bit of the good thing, the kids who need an intensive dose of it still may not get what they need to be successful. Intensity and duration are part of the package when remediation is prescribed for a student, and if there is not enough of it, or if it doesn't last for enough time, the student is still left behind. You can't be satisfied giving students twenty minutes a day if they need two hours.

We know the vital pieces that all students need in order to become literate. But teaching a little of each of those pieces separately without integrating all of them is a disservice because some students can't do the integrating on their own. Being independent with a small piece of reading skill isn't enough when kids still can't read functionally. Teaching kids to use skills functionally is difficult for teachers who haven't been taught to do that, and it takes a long time. You can't do it in twenty minutes a day.

Pop Quiz #4

_____ grade is broadly viewed as the children's last chance. Those who are not on track by _____ grade have little chance of ever catching up.

      a.   Tenth; Twelfth

      b.   Second; Third

      c.   Eighth; Ninth

      d.   Fifth; Sixth

(Answer at the back of the book)

Arlene Sonday, Founding Fellow and first President of the Academy of Orton

Children cannot work on decoding at the same time that they are working on comprehension. They devote so much mental energy to figuring out the word, they can't hold on to the meaning of the sentence.

Chyanne Wellman

Joan Stoner, EdD, President of the Nebraska branch of the International Dyslexia Association

If a young kid goes to a swimming lesson and is able to do everything expected of him, he will want to go back. If he goes to soccer practice and is not successful and cannot kick the ball where it needs to go, he hangs on Mom or Dad's leg, and doesn't want to play anymore. If we structure our schools so that children are successful from day one, we will be in good shape. But I can tell you that by the 31st of October, those first graders know if they are going to make it in school or not, and they are already starting to do anything they can to distract the teacher from whatever it is that they can't do.

When you can't do something everybody else in the room can do, you give yourself the label of *dumb*. And the kids who have labeled themselves *dumb* are kids who are fearful of every new situation at school. There are fewer students with learning difficulties in their junior and senior years. They aren't there anymore. They have chosen to leave school.

Arlene Sonday, Founding Fellow and first President of the Academy of Orton

Most of us who are really good readers and writers have strategies we are not even aware of. When we write the word Wednesday, we'll say to ourselves, *Wed-nes-day.* We're segmenting automatically. We find that when we're working with children with dyslexia, we have to directly teach them how to segment. We have to teach them the rules because they don't do it automatically.

There was a young man I tutored who came to the word *saltine.* We had worked on the suffix -*ine*, so he knew it: -*ine* as in *masculine* and *feminine*, -*ine* as in *machine* and *magazine*, and -*ine* as in *turpentine* and *valentine*. So he tried the first sound, and it didn't make sense to him, but as he got to the -*ine* in *saltine*, he said it in such a way that I believed he understood it. And I asked him, thinking I was a really good teacher to have brought him so far, "Well, what is a saltine?" He looked up and said, "That's when you hit somebody." I expected a low-level response, and he gave me high. Sometimes when the student's answer doesn't make sense, it is because of what *you* have said to him. I realize that now, but many teachers may not.

Mara Felman
The Kildonan School, Amenia, New York

Public school is supposed to help the masses learn, but all it does is drown the individual. Label = one word to describe a person, and comes with connotations about who he or she is as a whole: Smart. Dumb. Nice. Mean. Happy. Sad. Dyslexic. At Kildonan, they understand that we can't be summed up in one word. We are complex individuals. I am told I have an extraordinary ability to understand and apply the language of mathematics. I have a passion for the subject, and enjoy solving increasingly complex problems.

7
What Could School Be Like for Dyslexics?

Such a different environment is like going to another country, and it is the first chance many children have to believe in themselves and to feel that they can learn.
Joyce Pickering

Harvey,

What do you say?

I believe the Montessori schools are great. More teachers working with smaller groups of kids are the way to go. Seriously, why do we give teachers such a rough job when they have responsibility for teaching our greatest resources, our kids? There are so many kids in a typical classroom, and they come with so many differences. Each is a unique learner, but how can one teacher keep track of what each one needs? It's absurd. We need to reduce class size and respect the student. Who is this kid? What can he do, and what can't he do? Let's honor the strengths and work on the weaknesses. How can we improve his deficits while we notice and respect what he's good at, and keep him believing in himself? That's the million-dollar question.

Early intervention is key for a child with a learning difference. Schools are getting better at identifying issues earlier, but they still have a long way to go. It wasn't until the late '70s that certain laws were passed to help guys like me with learning disabilities. But by that time, I was seventeen years old. I was already a juvenile delinquent. Special education laws are not going to help a seventeen-year-old kid with a lot of learning differences who has failed in the public school system and already has a reputation in a small town of being a troublemaker. All of the king's horses and all the king's men are not going to help that kid.

Now we are learning to identify children early, diagnose the specific learning disability, and prescribe a research-based education program early on. This is what early intervention is all about, and it can make a positive difference in a child's education. My own daughter is the perfect example of it. She was identified with dyslexia at an early age and given scientifically proven, Orton-Gillingham-based early intervention. Now she is doing fine in school.

There are so many more compensating mechanisms available to students. Computers. Spell check. It's everywhere, on text messages and emails. If you're dysgraphic and can't write words very well, you might never have to hold a pencil again. You just type, and your work looks fine. Text-to-speech software reads to you, and reads back to you what you write. Technology to support the needs of dyslexic brains keeps getting better and better. Or you can do as I do, and surround yourself with people who can spell better and type faster. I lose my train of thought when I type, and prefer to be the thinker rather than the typer.

Brain Specialists,
What do you say?

Gordon Sherman, PhD, Executive Director of Newgrange School and Education Center

We know about cerebrodiversity where everyone comes in with a different approach to learning and with different processing capabilities. The best schools teach to the individual children, and don't force them to learn under one set of circumstances.

It is wonderful to see a student develop self-awareness: *I process information differently. This isn't about me being stupid. It isn't about me being lazy. It's about me finding an area where I can really fly.*

Now, is the problem dyslexia or dysteachia? We need to go back to the teaching colleges and make sure they are teaching teachers the most effective way for all students to learn to read. If it is too late for someone out there in the field, we need to help teachers get certified in structured language programs through workshops, to help them understand that there is a very powerful way to teach reading, and it may not be the way they learned in college. Principals need to understand this, too. There are major differences in the way students process information, and daily instruction must provide multiple ways for students to learn.

Elaina Saracino

When a tenth grader, eleventh grader, or twelfth grader comes to the Newgrange School, we often see that they have gone through their school career with a label they don't really understand. They haven't been offered appropriate remediation, and their self-esteem is very low. They think they are not smart, that something is very wrong with them. They've been called lazy, *Why don't you try harder?* But they know they've been trying as hard as they possibly can.

On the reverse side, when we get students in second, third, even fourth grade and explain to them what the issues are, they start to see that with effective instruction success is possible: *Hey, I can do this stuff!* We can save those kids from losing their self-esteem, and that is where early intervention is key.

Carolyn Cowen, Executive Director, Carroll School Center for
Innovative Education

Early intervention is important because that is when the human brain
is most responsive to input on the structure of language. Remediation
is much more powerful at an early age. In a similar way, a young child
can more easily learn a second language. It is the same concept of
brain plasticity. There is a lot of time lost waiting until third grade
or so to remediate a reading difficulty. Now we know so much more
about what to look for, and we can screen kids much earlier. We can
catch them in pre-K.

Gordon Sherman, PhD, Executive Director of Newgrange School and
Education Center

It is less costly for schools to screen for dyslexia in the earliest grades,
and put in place the proper educational procedures early on. Those
children may struggle somewhat, but they will become readers. It is
far more expensive to remediate when you discover that an eleventh
grader is dyslexic. At this point, many school systems have not yet
developed this awareness. It is better than it was ten, twenty years
ago, but we have a long, long way to go. And maybe a documentary
like this will help.

And should we put 90 percent of our time into remediation, or
should we try a more forward-thinking approach and come up with
a curriculum that really matches what these brains are capable of? I
don't know of many schools really pushing the idea that we need to
reformulate our approach to teaching people with dyslexia.

Dyslexics,

What do you say?

Stephen J. Cannell, Writer, Producer

I always wanted to be a writer. Always. In my high-school yearbook, under **Ambition**, it says: *Author.* Why did I insist on that that when I was flunking English? It's what I always wanted to be. So I took this creative writing course in my sophomore year at University of Oregon. Ralph Salisbury was the instructor – great, great guy, and still my friend. I always asked my new professors about their policy on misspellings, and if one said, "Well, three misspellings is a flunk," then I'd drop the course, but Ralph said, "Ah, Steve. This is a writing class. If you can spell something phonetically, I can get through that." And then he said the most incredible thing anybody had ever said to me in all the years I had been in school: "I want you to make me a promise. I want you to promise to use all the words that you know, not just the ones you think you can spell."

Before, if I needed the word *conspicuous* (which I can't spell), I would write *easy to see* (which I can spell). But that just isn't as good a way to say it. I had a good vocabulary anyway, and now all of a sudden, I had it available to me, to use in my writing.

Luke Bornheimer, Graduate of The Forman School

I first came into Wendy Welshans's class at The Forman School fixed on the idea that I had to write down everything that she wrote on the board. But she gave the class a different spin, and it was so nice to see that this wasn't another situation where I had to struggle just to copy exactly what she said. She forced us to think in different ways, and by the end of the year, it was pretty amazing.

Billy Bob Thornton, Musician, Actor, and Filmmaker

I tell people that I'm in the Hall of Fame for the Learning Disabled. And they start laughing, right? They think I'm joking. But seriously, it's at the Lab School in Washington, DC, with plaques on the wall, the whole deal.

Before the induction ceremony, they took me around to see some classes. In a history class, the kids were all dressed up, one like Shakespeare, one like Leonardo da Vinci, and so on. I could tell this was something that focused them. This was fun. I liked this. The next thing you know, the kids were learning because they were interested. It wasn't just some guy's name on a page. The guy came to life, so it felt like they were involved in the actual events. Hey, there's an idea, make school interesting. I thought, *Well, why don't they do this in school every minute – even with kids who don't have dyslexia?*

That's why I believe in these looser, more artistic schools where they encourage kids in the directions that they're interested in rather than limiting them to the five basic subjects. It's like I told that teacher years ago, when she said I had to learn algebra because I might want to be a building engineer someday. I said, "Ma'am, I promise you with all my heart and soul, I'm never going to want to be a building engineer."

When a teacher has one of those kids with his head up in the clouds, I think she should investigate what that kid is thinking: *Let me get up there in the stratosphere where this kid operates, and I'll find what this is all about. Then I'll teach him more of that,* as opposed to forcing a square peg into a round hole. That's the way I look at it.

Luke Bornheimer, Graduate of The Forman School

I think we need to educate people about learning differences so they don't see them as a disability but as just another way of learning. A big thing at our school is to treat learning differently as normal, and to work with it instead of acting like there's something wrong with you.

Tom West, Author

Teachers have required that all the dyslexics do things the way the teacher is doing them. But I'm saying we should be more assertive and expect teachers to understand the talents that dyslexics have, even when the teachers don't have those talents themselves.

Billy Bob Thornton, Musician, Actor, and Filmmaker

I wanted to be a rock 'n' roll star and a baseball player. I didn't care anything about acting. But I thought, *Hey – drama class – there are chicks in there, and maybe I'll get something above a C in at least one subject.* And sure enough, all that was true. My drama teacher, a woman named Maude Treadway, came up to me after class one day and said, "Listen, most people are just in this class to goof off and have a break from the hard subjects, but I think you can really do this. I think you could actually become very successful with this in the future." This was just a little town in Arkansas, but I listened to her, and got the starring role in the senior play.

And she said, "I'm going to have you start writing your own scenes. We're going to improvise. I want you to do your own scenes and monologues." And she actually let me direct people in the class. It was the first time in my life in an organized, institutional setting where somebody ever said, *Wow, you're good at this, and I'm going to let you do what you want.* That's what I did, and it turned out to be amazing. I would get up there and do monologues just off the top of my head.

I made a movie called *Sling Blade* in 1994. When I first wrote that movie, I didn't actually write anything down. There's an eight or nine minute monologue in the beginning of the movie. And when I used to do it onstage in a theater, I didn't have it written down anywhere. It was all in my head.

Kyle Morrissey, Graduate of The Kildonan School

My mother didn't want me to go to our public middle school, which didn't have much of a program for people with reading difficulties. So we looked around and found The Kildonan School. I came in the sixth grade, and I was only at a second grade reading level. But that year I read my first official book, all by myself. That was when I was thirteen. I've come a long way since then. Now I am thinking about going to college soon.

A great thing about Kildonan is that they coordinate trips for the students in tenth, eleventh, and twelfth grades. The trips help us to get to know each other better and become more of a community.

Sarah Joy Brown, Emmy Award-winning actress

In my senior year of high school at Hamilton Academy of Music, my performing arts teacher handed back a paper I had written. It looked like a war zone. As my teachers always did, he had taken his red pen and outlined everything I had misspelled and every bit of incorrect punctuation, but this was different. He gave me an A. When I asked him why, with every third word misspelled, he had given me an A, he said, "Because you're really brilliant. You're a great writer, but you're dyslexic. I don't think I should grade you down for that. "

And *ding*—a bell rang that started my journey. He saw my dyslexia, and he was the first person to make sense of it for me, just by giving it an A.

Kim Bucciantini, Graduate of The Forman School

If you want to help kids, you have to sit down with them one-on-one. You have to understand that if they can't write stuff by hand, then they have to type it, no matter what. You have to understand that you can't treat them like any other students because they are not like any other students. They need one-on-one time, and they need extra support.

Luke Bornheimer, Graduate of The Forman School

A lot us here at school have friends at home who think, *Oh, you have less homework. You get more time. You have it easier. You get anything you need to succeed, blah, blah, blah.* We might need more time. We might need a smaller class. And if that is what it takes for us to learn, then I don't see the reason why we shouldn't be allowed to have that. It's kind of silly that people set this one standard for how you should learn and one type of environment for successful schooling. I think what The Forman School does is show that any kids can succeed if they find the environment that works for them and if they find the thing that really intrigues and motivates them.

Jonathan Marhaba
Frostig Center, Pasadena, California

I had no friends, and was called stupid, retarded and other names. I spent countless hours doing school to keep up. But at the Frostig Center, when I am working on something and ask a teacher for help or to give me their opinion on my work, they come

and do it. I understand people who only associate with their own crowd. I am able to do so well as an actor and an artist because I have been alienated for many years and have spent some time in a certain crowd that helped my personality evolve.

Parents,

What do you say?

Carol Hill, Parent and educational advocate for dyslexics

Time and time again, reading specialists/special education teachers have told me they knew nothing of research-based, effective methods for teaching all children to read until they searched on their own later in their careers. Our teachers in America simply don't know what they don't know. It is only after a long, personal journey and firsthand experience that teachers come to understand the complexities of working with dyslexic students. Even when local districts provide mentoring from tenured teachers, often those tenured teachers continue to promote methods they think have been working all these years, although current research tells us they have been ineffective for many, many students.

But I have witnessed successful instruction by a thoroughly trained teacher. It is an uplifting and illuminating experience. It looks like the most natural approach in the world. No expensive materials are used. No fancy gadgets or technology are purchased. But the teacher has become a teaching artist and coach. When you see the trained teacher using methods to double-check that a student understands, you see that nothing is left to chance. A student's reliance on a strong intellect and an ability to simply memorize do not mislead this type of trained teacher. If our local classroom teachers, reading specialists, and special education teachers could be influenced to pursue this scientific approach, they would see for themselves the great joy it creates in a student who is finally returning to confidence and hope.

Now my son is blossoming in a school that specializes in teaching children with dyslexia. Everything is presented for learning in a multisensory way. Students build a Zen garden, incorporating lessons in geometry, weight, measurement, and culture. After accomplishing so much with teamwork, they are very proud of the end product. And that's just math class. It is understood that my son is intelligent, and he has access to pens that can record and play back as he writes, computer programs, memory chips, and planners. He is in the first generation of students who use these devices as they would a wheelchair. At this school, they accommodate and let his quick-thinking brain solve problems.

Carole Bellew, Parent of Luke Bornheimer

It's very hard to leave your thirteen-year-old at boarding school, but I could do nothing more for him, and he needed outside help. It's been four years, and I couldn't ask for any more than he has gotten here. I have been asked by Luke's elementary school to speak with parents about learning disabilities and what to do for their children, because Luke has had such success at Forman. I am determined to try to share some of what Luke has experienced here in hopes that schools can do a better job for other kids.

Voncille Wright, Parent of Jo'Von Wright

We sent Jo'Von to a small independent school in Connecticut. It made all the difference in the world. She was a flower waiting to come alive and bloom. She moved up three grade levels in reading in one year because she was able to utilize the techniques they taught her. There, she began to develop the self-confidence to stand on her own two feet, but when she outgrew that school, we came to The Forman School. At that time, we had two other children in college, but we decided that Jo'Von's education was one of the most important things that we could do, and we made some financial sacrifices.

This school has done marvelous things for Jo'Von. She has excelled in the theater. She was elected dorm leader this year. She has gotten a couple of scholarships, and she is looking at some very serious colleges.

Carol Hill, Parent and educational advocate for dyslexics

One of the problems I have seen in public schools is when children who struggle move on to the next grade without a system in place to double-check their current abilities as they enter a new class. I have suggested to a parochial school in Westchester, New York, that they create a pilot program where teachers would participate in Orton-Gillingham training and a practicum within their building. Then they could start opening up some parochial schools that have been closed down, have local districts send children for specialized, multisensory instruction for three years at a time, and then incorporate them back into the district. I'm hoping they take me up on it.

Genevieve Greer
Churchill Center and School, St. Louis, Missouri

I have written a book called Belle's Dyslexia. It is more like a children's book than an adult book. And it might interest both parents and children who have to deal with dyslexia. I have never been in public school, but I know that there are lots of kids

like Belle, who have hard times at school because of their dyslexia. "I'm too sick to go to school all week," said Belle. This was true, in a way, because she was sick OF school. "I don't think you are sick," said her mother. Belle decided to pull out her first grade trick. Her face turned yellow, green, and then hot pink while she concentrated on something really hard. If she concentrated on something really, really gross, she could actually make herself vomit! Her mother never knew this was actually a trick!

Teachers,

What do you say?

Joyce Pickering, SLC/CCC, CALT, QI, Hum D, Executive Director Emeritus of Shelton School

Picture this: you're in a school where you are experiencing no success, hour after hour, day after day. People there do not understand why you can't succeed and even say to you, "I know you can do this. You're an intelligent kid. You can do better if you try harder." But you are trying the hardest you can, sometimes much harder than the other kids. Still can't do it. You begin to worry more and more about yourself. *What's wrong with me?* Your parents don't understand it either, and you feel like you are down in a well, all by yourself.

Then you enter a school where dyslexia is understood. Every teacher has the skills to help you, and other children with your same difficulties know how it feels. Such a different environment is like going to another country, and it is the first chance many children have to believe in themselves and to feel that they can learn.

Isaiah Stockdale

Dana Blackhurst, Headmaster, Camperdown Academy

I tell kids three important things: "I know you can do it, I won't give up on you, and I'm right behind you." And that doesn't mean love taps. That means, *I'll see you Saturday morning, bucko, right here in my class.* If they trust you, you can say that.

That's why they have practices in sports. *Let's throw this at 'em. Let's throw this at 'em. Let's see how our team works under adversity.* Kids in school have to handle adversity but in a safe environment. That's why I plan it out way ahead of time.

Diana Hanbury King, Founder of The Kildonan School

When I was teaching at Sidwell Friends, Anna Gillingham had a program called the Problem Prevention Program. She carefully screened kindergarteners herself. Any child she considered at risk was placed in one of several first grades with a totally Orton-Gillingham approach, completely phonetic with cursive writing from the beginning. And that group was kept together until the end of fourth grade, when she tested them again. She found them on a par with the population from the regular classroom, except in spelling. The children who had been at risk were better in spelling. And of course, they were undamaged. They never had to fail. They never had to see themselves as stupid. That's a simple program.

I remember thinking at the time that it would surely be replicated in every public school, and there would be no need for remediation. But it never happened. That was in 1951 or '52, a long time ago. We've known how to fix these problems for a long time. But it requires that teachers be trained, and that the training take place in colleges where they are still embracing the whole-word approach.

Robin Winternitz, Dyslexia advocate and educational consultant

Home schooling is on the rise. After a school does not meet a child's particular needs, some parents across the country are stepping up and pulling their children out to help them get back that desire to learn. They can home school until the child graduates, or for one or two years, or even just for half a semester. Each state has its own guidelines.

Home schooling is completely different than it was years ago. We used to think it was just for religious families or hippies, but now there are all kinds of people doing it from laborers to doctors. Some parents are realizing that they do not have to provide the actual instruction for their children themselves, but they can contract out to tutors, or find umbrella groups that will teach classes. Many community colleges have also jumped on the bandwagon and are offering classes to home schoolers.

Angelica Goodhue

Joan Stoner, EdD, President of the Nebraska branch of the International Dyslexia Association

In middle school, high school, and college, when students can't figure out a word and can't spell it, they are reluctant to turn in written assignments because it seems better to be in trouble for not turning in work than to feel really stupid. We encourage them to spell the best they can, underline the words they aren't sure of, and ask someone they can trust to help them fix the misspellings. Everybody says, *Yeah, a computer can do that for you,* but a computer will not pick up a word that has multiple meanings. It could be spelled correctly but not for that particular sentence.

These students have such a struggle taking notes and writing down words they can't spell while they are listening to and processing what the professor is saying, and then trying to make sense of the notes later. Professors have been reluctant to make their notes available to students, but when people who know their own learning strengths and limitations have started to go back to school, they tell the instructors, "I can't watch what you're doing with the pictures and graphs and take notes at the same time," and they ask for copies of the professor's notes. They know they are not being lazy. This has influenced the practice of professors providing their notes in the bookstore where students can buy them and have lecture notes clearly written out so they can pay attention to what they are seeing and hearing. It's been wonderful for them.

Joyce Pickering, SLC/CCC, CALT, QI, Hum D, Executive Director Emeritus of Shelton School

We start with children where they are. Eventually, some will even exceed average performance in a grade level, some will reach grade level performance, and some will improve but not reach grade level. Even then, once children have an understanding of their learning differences and the coping skills and strategies that help them learn, we start using all kinds of assistive technology, so that children who might have felt they are terrible failures can be functional. That's what we're after – that they be functional, in the mainstream, in college, and in life.

Wendy Welshans, Environmental Science Teacher, The Forman School

When we began the Rainforest Project at The Forman School, people said, "Oh, you take the kids to Costa Rica. That's a nice vacation." But it's not a vacation at all. These kids know their work is important. They sign up knowing that their data will be used, and their project is going to make a difference. They're just itching to start their projects and can't wait to get there. They know they have limited time, and they want to make their discoveries, test out their theories, and test their new traps or whatever they have built.

We're building new extraction devices for spider silk, new traps to isolate poisonous snakes, and new collection devices to capture scorpions and bullet ants so that people can stay out of harm's way. We have handy dandy toothbrush tweezers that are three feet long PVC pipes that have children's toothbrushes in the ends. They're attached at the bottom with a piece of wood, and we can walk up to any scorpion from three feet away, grab it tightly with the toothbrushes without harming it, and put it in the bucket for further identification. These work very well. We've taken little Hoover vacuum cleaners and attached containers with tubes to throw in our packs. With the little vacuums, we can load these containers with deadly things very easily and very carefully. It's a collaboration of the students coming up with these ideas and me thinking about what might work better over time.

A lot of the kids who apply during their junior year to participate in this project in their senior year have been waiting for a chance since their freshman or sophomore year. Some of them have been told by siblings about the project. Sometimes their siblings wish they could have gone, but they didn't have the motivation or the grades to be able to do it.

But it is not necessarily all about grades. We aren't looking for straight-A students. I could take some C students as long as I saw they had amazing problem-solving capabilities and the motivation to improve their critical thinking skills and really make a difference. We look for critical thinking that is way beyond that of a linear thinking peer. We ask the students questions in the interview that allow us to know if they have this critical thinking beast at their core, waiting to break out.

Evelyn Russo, PhD, Haskins Laboratories Literacy Initiative

Early on, we try to hook children into paying attention to the sounds of our language. Rhymes don't predict reading success, but they do help make the child aware that the words coming out of our mouths are made up of sounds. And that's the ticket to pre-K. The concept is so cognitively challenging and so abstract that using a tool like the puppet Sonar makes it more apparent and concrete, not to mention fun and engaging.

Our kindergarteners know all of the alphabet, all of the diagraphs, and they can hear blends at the beginning and at the ends of words. They know closed and open syllables. There are basically six syllable types, and if you know them, you can decode at least 80 percent of the words in our language. All of our first graders can read all the syllable types. In second grade, we make sure they can spell all of these patterns. Reading is partial knowledge of the structure of our language, but spelling is complete mastery and understanding, and that's what we are shooting for.

Here in the classroom, every teacher is doing everything in her power to help kids to become aware of sounds. We play lots of games, we make it fun and glittery, we offer many chances to respond, and the kids love to practice, practice, practice. And here's the remarkable piece: in trying to prevent failure, we have added more success and moved kids so much further that I ever thought possible.

We teach all children this way, whether they are dyslexic or not, because we think that we are going to be more successful that way. We are going to be more explicit, we are going to be more systematic, and we are going to have a lot of fun doing it. We hope to prevent failure, and that is why we teach this way to everyone who comes through our doors.

But we also work on inference, vocabulary, and narrative development because they are just as crucial. Word attack skills are very important for kids to become independent readers, but before they have the skills to read anything, we still have to work on comprehension, and we do that early on through listening comprehension.

Some schools are afraid of the word *dyslexia*, and I have absolutely no idea what they are thinking. All I am trying to do is offer every single child the best chance possible to discover the gift of reading. The statistics on how many people can't read are staggering to me, and I would like to do something about that. Even though reading is one of the most complex things that the brain does, I think that when we're informed by research and spend time working with students, we can find a way to make it happen.

These children are going to be successful. They are going to be literate, and they are going to be effective communicators. They are going to be able to understand material that they read, and they are going to be able to effectively articulate their thoughts.

Although students may not be able to read some material on their own, there are still many things they want to know about, so each child can listen to recorded books that are two, three, or four years above their actual reading ability. Here, fabulous readers like Jim Dale and Lynn Redgrave read to them. We have text for students to decode that they can easily lift off the page themselves, and we have specialized text to help with spelling, text to increase vocabulary, and text for inferencing because the decodables are not as complex. Everything has its purpose, and our teachers know this.

Haskins people are sometimes accused of mainly worrying about word attack skills, or phonemic awareness, or the code, and *then* fluency and comprehension. But no, we are just as concerned with increasing vocabulary, and inferencing, and comprehension.

We use Brady the puppet to help reveal story grammar or all the parts of stories. We also work on the microstructure of language and the language kids need to tell about the story parts. Lots of times in stories a critical-thinking triangle is not explicit, so we have to use our inferencing skills. If we spot one piece, we can try to figure out the other pieces.

This is all based on the work of Maryellen Moreau and *Mindwings*. She's been part of our Mastering Reading staff development and has helped us with the background knowledge piece. For the reading to make sense, kids need to have some information about it in their background knowledge backpack, so to say. Because how do you infer? You use what you know about the world. But you don't have to go to the Peabody Museum to increase your background knowledge; you just have to think about how you would react in your own life experiences.

When we read books to pre-K children and ask them to retell the story, we often see that they are in an action sequence stage of narrative development. We try to move them to the next level where they can spot an initiating event. Then we want them to be able to spot feelings and plans, then spot attempts to carry out a plan, and then to ask themselves if the plan was successful. And we want them to learn how to describe the feelings of the characters at the end, at the resolution. We have to make this apparent to kids and put it in their story schema, in their background knowledge, so they can communicate more effectively and at a more complex level.

We can take what looks to be a very simple story and help young children think critically about it, talk about it, and find the parts that have to do with higher-level thinking. Then, when they are capable of lifting the words off the page by themselves, there is a happy meeting of the kids who have great word attack skills but difficulty with inferencing, and the kids who aren't using sounds to make sense of the code but have great inferencing ability in their listening comprehension.

We are careful to equip kids with specific strategies to lift words off the page because by third or fourth grade, they suddenly are confronted with ten thousand words that they've never seen before, and memorizing new words isn't going to cut it. We also are careful to equip kids to be able to make inferences and progress in their narrative development. We begin with narrative development because it is easier, but we also teach them about expository and nonfiction text because that is even more complicated. As the saying goes, in the beginning, from pre-K to grade three, children learn to read. From grade four on, they must read to learn. So we equip them with the knowledge and skills they will need.

I wish reading were magical! I wish, but you know what? We know how to teach kids to read better, and it's not by magic. It's by teacher knowledge.

Emily Bruder
Friendship School, Eldersburg, Maryland

At my old school, people teased me because I couldn't read a thing. One of my best experiences at Friendship School was when I finished the Orton-Gillingham book in tutoring class. It took me about two years. I wrote "If I Could Fly" in my creative writing journal at school. I like to take risks with my writing.

If I Could Fly

If I could fly across the world
I would do it in a night.
If I could flutter about the stars
I would do it in one try.

If I could dance with the planets
If my soul could fly in the air
It would, it would, it would.

I can only wish and try with my
Heart's desire when I am up there.
I am so small compared to up there.
I'll just sit here
Tonight.

8
What Treatments Are Effective for Dyslexia?

A multisensory language program using sequential order and lots of repetition is the most effective way to build different pathways in the brain so that it is easier to process sounds and language.
Linda Selvin

Harvey,
What do you say?

Many people wish they could cure their dyslexia or find a way to make their children normal in school. But what is so great about normal? Should normal also be cured? I think normal gets us into a lot more problems than dyslexia, so I don't think people should be worrying too much about cures. I think they should just be themselves.

I was a kid with a learning disability, but I believe I was disabled by the system. If the teachers couldn't teach me, wasn't that a teaching disability? When teachers aim for the middle of the class, 20 percent of the kids on one end and 20 percent of kids on the other end probably aren't going to benefit from that kind of teaching. But there are some research-validated methods, like ones we see at Hamden Hall in the film, where all the kids learn because particular methods are used to reach them all. That's your multisensory education.

People who get training in Orton-Gillingham methods are like Jedis. There are different levels: I believe you start off with thirty hours of training and become an associate, and the trainings continue on and on through hundreds of hours to the level of an Orton fellow. More and more people are getting Orton-Gillingham training because it works.

I have met many Orton fellows who have a brother or sister who was really smart, but failed in the school system. Or a spouse realizes that a partner is smart and capable, but has dyslexia. Or they give birth to a child who does very well until reading instruction begins in school. This firsthand experience can motivate people to become educators and get this special training. They want to help make a change.

I don't get asked this very often, but I actually do have a regret. During most of my life, I have lived about an hour's drive away from The Kildonan School – an hour away from Diana King. She has successfully taught people with the most severe dyslexia, and I think she could have changed my life. Of course I will always have dyslexia, and I will always think the way I think, but what I regret is not being remediated early on by a teacher like Diana King. If I could have avoided the school nightmare, and had an expert teacher teach me to read as a child, I think I could be so much more productive now. I could write more and more quickly. I would hang on to my creativity, but I would just be able to accomplish much more. That would have been nice.

Ed. Note: In 2011, Harvey began weekly remediation with Diana King.

Brain Specialists,

What do you say?

Ken Pugh, PhD, President and Director of Research, Haskins Laboratories

Often data don't conform themselves to our naive hypotheses, but we start with a premise that is supported by many, many years of behavioral research. And then we continue to explore the brain to see if in fact we need more rich and detailed accounts. And right now, there are many theories out there, and we are aware of them, and we will test them all. We start from our own hypotheses, but we fully expect, as in all science, that our puny expectations will be violated by the real world. But that's where we start.

Gordon Sherman, PhD, Executive Director of Newgrange School and Education Center

Early intervention is so critical because it is about not wasting time. But more importantly, it's about taking advantage of the incredible plasticity of the brain - the ability of the brain to change under different environmental conditions. That plasticity is at really high levels from birth up to the age of eight or so, and that is when we need to make sure we're identifying and remediating dyslexia. Actually, the best time to identify is at kindergarten or before. If you wait, plasticity is reduced, so remediation is going to take longer and be more frustrating.

Guinevere Eden, PhD, Past President, International Dyslexia Association

There are things we just don't know yet. As scientists, we work from models and theories, and dyslexia is so complicated that one theory doesn't explain everything. People are now beginning to use different types of tools and do more integrated, more interdisciplinary work where they try to combine brain imaging with behavior and genetics. Once we pull all of those together, I think we will know much more about the causes of dyslexia. We still have a long way to go in understanding which child benefits from which intervention. When you go buy some medication because you have a headache, you don't want to fuss around and think about which pill to take - the pink one or the blue one. That work has all been done by the scientific community and has gone though regulations to insure that there are benefits to that medication that outweigh any risks. We don't have that for reading interventions. Parents struggle to pull together the research, and they struggle to interpret the research and pin it to their particular situation.

There is work going on now at the U.S. Department of Education in the What Works Clearinghouse to understand research-based interventions that are effective: *What are the strengths of those studies? What are the weaknesses? What do we still need to do?* It's a difficult problem, but it needs to be tackled so that when you recognize that you have a child with a reading problem, you can then very quickly make a decision about the course of action. You don't want to feel that you are using your own child as a guinea pig, taking him from one intervention to the next, and mortgaging your house in the process.

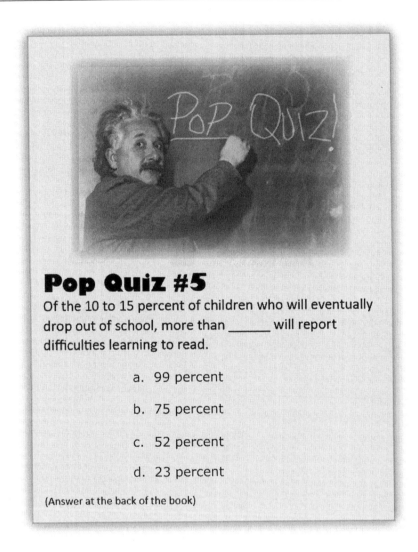

Pop Quiz #5

Of the 10 to 15 percent of children who will eventually drop out of school, more than _____ will report difficulties learning to read.

    a. 99 percent

    b. 75 percent

    c. 52 percent

    d. 23 percent

(Answer at the back of the book)

Gordon Sherman, PhD, Executive Director of Newgrange School and Education Center

Dyslexia is a term that has value, but it is not very specific. We see weaknesses and strengths in different areas. There is some controversy about this, but it seems that most people with dyslexia have phonemic awareness and phonological processing issues. But there may be some people diagnosed with dyslexia who have issues in the orthographic domain. Spend some time in a school for dyslexics, and that becomes very clear. That said, a multisensory, structured-language program works best for students with dyslexia. It is the best way to teach them how to read. There are a lot of alternate therapies out there, but nothing has been shown to work like these multisensory techniques. So that's advice to parents, too. If they are going to put their attention, energy, and money anywhere, that's the place to put it.

Sylvia O. Richardson, MD, Past President, Orton Dyslexia Society

A child learns spoken language through a multisensory avenue: through the eye, watching Mom and how she looks forming all those words that come out of her mouth; through the ear, learning the melody and intonation, or prosody, of his own language; and through the muscles, practicing forming and babbling approximations of words until he is able to communicate with speech. That's how children learn spoken language, and that's how children with dyslexia best learn written language: utilizing all the senses, not just the eyes or ears.

Che Kan Leong, PhD, Research Professor Emeritus, University of Saskatchewan

My main interest is cross-language research, where we talk about dyslexia and how it is and isn't different across languages that have different characteristics, such as Japanese or Chinese, which are vastly different from English in written and spoken form.

I believe the real breakthroughs in dyslexia will come from the biological sciences. With fMRI, scientists will be able to link behavioral, linguistic, cognitive, and biological aspects. With this information, society will gain a deeper understanding of dyslexia, and fewer people will be saying, "Oh, this child is just too lazy," or, "He doesn't do his work."

In the last analysis, everything comes back to teaching. Teachers, principals, and other educators must have a better understanding of dyslexia and find alternative methods to reach children.

People in places such as Hong Kong and Taiwan are very conscious of tests and examinations. With my medical colleagues, I have been working through the Examination Authority in China to make sure that individuals with dyslexia have proper accommodations on their examinations. I give a lot of credit to my colleagues and to parents who fight for better services. Exciting changes are coming to a part of the world where, for a long time, people simply denied that there was such a condition as dyslexia.

David Lord
Triad Academy, Winston-Salem, North Carolina

While we were at the Renaissance Fair on a field trip, I saw everything that my teachers had taught me about the Renaissance and the Middle Ages. They teach without a lot of words. In public school, there were always tests. I felt stupid because it was hard for me to do well. I always got D's and F's. I am told that I have extraordinary talent in the visual arts, and become absorbed in my superb attention to detail in my artwork.

Guinevere Eden, PhD, Past President, International Dyslexia Association

A number of techniques have been around since the 1970s that allow us to generate an image of the brain or another part of the body. In one technique, a radioactive tracer is injected and taken up in the body. It goes up to the brain and shows us where there is an increase of blood flow to a particular area. That tells us where the neurons are working.

With functional magnetic resonance imaging, or fMRI, we don't have to inject a tracer. The functional piece is fairly new, discovered in the early 1990s. With additional hardware and software, it tells us where there are areas of increased oxygen presence. When the neurons are busy, they need more oxygen delivered so they can function, and it turns out that the hemoglobin molecule in our blood sends a slightly different signal when it is carrying oxygen. This shows up differently on the image. We use that information to infer where the brain is working, where the neurons are active. This is a technique that gives us a window into the brain, based on the physiology relationships that we know. It has become extremely useful in studies that examine how the brain is organized for different functions.

The fMRI is noninvasive, and with it we have the opportunity to look at children. It would be unethical to use invasive techniques with children, but because we're not injecting anything, we have lots of interested volunteers. Now we're getting closer to the real problem, and we're not just limited to asking questions about adults. We can look at children at the very moment it becomes clear that they're struggling readers. That's where we can learn a lot using fMRI.

The usual reason people have fMRI's done is to participate in a study. They volunteer their time to help scientists collect data to increase their knowledge about the brain. It may change with time, but right now, we use the fMRI as a tool that allows us to map out areas that are involved with reading, phonemic awareness, and semantic processing. We can see what happens in the brains of readers when they are asked to do a number of diverse tasks.

The fMRI is a research tool, not a diagnostic tool. The signal we measure is a 10 percent change in brain response to a stimulus that we present to a person. We are not at the stage yet where we have sufficient power to say something diagnostic about an individual. But ask me in a year, and I think things may change. This is a rapidly advancing field.

Ken Pugh, PhD, President and Director of Research, Haskins Laboratories

While fMRI and positron emission tomography, or PET scans, give us information about where things are happening, they provide very weak information about timing. But electroencephalography, or EEG, and magnetoencephalography, or MEG, can provide information about real-time electrical activity in different parts of the brain.

Diffusion tensor imaging, or DTI, allows us to actually image the axonal tracks that connect one part of the brain to another through white matter. This allows us to see how different parts are wired relative to one another.

Finally, there is another type of imaging called magnetic resonance spectroscopy, or MRS, where we can use brain imaging to measure the concentrations of different chemicals and agents that are critical to learning in different parts of the brain.

Lots of advances in physics and biomedicine allow cognitive neuroscience researchers to study the structure, the function or the chemistry of the brain, to help them better understand individual differences in cognitive development.

Steve Frost, PhD, Senior Scientist, Haskins Laboratories

We have a fascinating study right now that is a thing of beauty. It consists of the presentation of a word and a reaction. We would expect that good readers get faster and more accurate at it, and they do, but we see that poor readers also get faster and more accurate. However, brain activation in reading-related sites is actually reduced in good readers. We think this is because the more they see words, the more efficient they get at processing them.

In contrast, brain activation is increased in dyslexic readers, and they actually start activating the same sites that the good readers used – sites that were not activated before they got good at this task. One of the big questions about dyslexia has been whether the typical reading areas in the brain are broken, or just weak in some way, yet able to be used with some intervention. This suggests for dyslexic, particularly adolescent, readers, who have a real history of doing things wrong, that they *can* get the reading machinery to start working.

We continue to try to understand how to help a person with dyslexia improve reading performance. It has been suggested that dyslexic readers use different parts of the brain, and so with intervention, those different parts of the brain may just work better. But what we are seeing now is that when they start reading better, they start using the same areas as good readers, which leads us back to that idea that the problem is a weakness, not a break, in the language circuitry. This has a lot of implications for remediating a reading disability. It is neat stuff.

Ken Pugh, PhD, President and Director of Research, Haskins Laboratories

Margie Gillis and her Early Reading Success program have been an effective model. At Haskins, we have evidence-based principles that have passed the scrutiny of careful research. But teachers need this information, and they don't often get it. Margie's program trains master teachers who then go and spend one year in a school to provide teachers with tools needed to help kids who struggle with reading and language.

Now, neurobiology is very sexy, and people really are interested in seeing those pictures of the brain, but there is a wealth of knowledge that's already in place that can be translated into the classroom. Right now, there is less information that teachers need to know from brain imaging and more that they need to know from years of careful behavioral research.

Yes, we are making real inroads into neurobiology, but the translational work is crucial to teachers. I would never say, "Oh, I found this thing in the left occipital temporal part of the brain, so now you should teach differently."

Richard Olson, PhD, Professor, Colorado Learning Disabilities Research Center

On the biological side, the hope is that what we learn about genetic influence will lead us to be able to change the rate at which a child learns. It might be possible to eventually develop a drug therapy that would improve the way the brain processes information and speeds it up in a way that makes learning to read more efficient.

However, if somebody with reading difficulties were to look at that as a possible option, he might say, "Well, I'm not sure I want you monkeying around with my brain. My life is fine as it is. Yes, it was kind of hard to learn to read, but that does not define me." I would imagine that many people with learning difficulties would not want that kind of intervention, and certainly people should have the right to make a decision like that.

I think there is a lot of promise for the future, including a better understanding of the biological basis of dyslexia, but I don't want to hold out the hope that we are soon going to have a genetic solution to the problem of reading difficulties. I'd say at this point, and probably for many years hence, it is going to be up to classroom teachers, reading teachers, special education teachers, and parents to provide the optimal environment for children to develop their reading skills in spite of their biological constraints.

Gabriel Suarez
The Gow School, South Wales, New York

My artwork was chosen to be on the cover of three Gow yearbooks and the school fundraiser cookbook. I love the feeling of brotherhood at Gow. Here, we all have the same disability and are not singled out for it. In another school, everyone looked at me funny because I was different. (I wrote upside down.) I didn't go to class after that, and studied art on my own that year.

Sylvia O. Richardson, MD, Past President, Orton Dyslexia Society

The term *dyslexia* originated in 1887 with a Stuttgart ophthalmologist, Professor Berlin, who used the term to describe individuals who had been brain injured, and as a result, were unable to read. That's how it started, and a great many neurologists became involved in this field. James Hinshelwood, who wrote a little book in 1917 called *Congenital Word Blindness*, was the first who said this was not the result of brain injury, but instead was the result of brain differences, and the treatment should be educational. He described a structured treatment he called the alphabet method.

Dr. Samuel Orton originally called the condition *strephosymbolia*, which means twisted symbols, but nobody could spell it or even say it, so that went out the window, and the term became *dyslexia*, which means either difficulty with the word, or difficulty with language, depending on whether you are looking for a Latin or Greek reference.

Dr. Orton worked with Anna Gillingham, a school psychologist, and Bessie Stillman, an educator, to develop a structured language program now called the Orton-Gillingham Method. Its great success has bred many offshoots and has created a lot of sibling rivalry. Now we have the Slingerland Institute, mostly on the West Coast. We have Project Read in the Great Lakes area. We've got Alphabetic Phonics, down in Texas primarily. We've got Spalding, which is based in Arizona and is widely used in the Southwest. And then there is the Wilson Language System, based in New England. I am probably missing some more, but they are all wonderfully effective methods that have been derived from Orton and Gillingham.

It all started with good old Hinshelwood but also with Maria Montessori, the first woman doctor in Italy. In 1907, she devised a multisensory program starting in preschool, with exercises in practical life to prepare children for end goals in reading, writing, and mathematics. The Montessori program weaves listening, looking, speaking, doing, and reading into one tapestry, and if children start in preschool with lots of sensory motor experiences, as well as the sounds and sights of the language, they will be ready when they hit school.

Richard Olson, PhD, Professor, Colorado Learning Disabilities Research Center

We have written grants to put computers in schools and designed programs to give children support while they are reading interesting stories that they have chosen. Students ask for feedback on difficult words, and the computer stores these words and gives the students practice on them later on. They also get questions every once in a while to see if they are tracking the meaning of the story. We tell the students that it is not just about reading words; it is also about understanding and enjoying what you are reading. What we find is that this additional practice of accurate reading on the computer can powerfully promote growth in word-reading skills and in comprehension and fluency as well.

Jon Shanahan

It doesn't mean that this displaces the teacher. But it does extend the reach of the teacher who has a classroom full of students and not enough time to sit down and provide that kind of feedback for each one of them. A computer represents a fairly cost-effective method of providing additional practice, and it frees up the teacher to promote motivation to read, to check on students' enjoyment of reading, and intervene when a student may be struggling with a particular task.

It is a real problem when the motivation to read fails for children with dyslexia because they have had such a struggle learning. They need more practice than the average child, but what often happens is that they get much less practice because they are so discouraged by the process. This is why I believe that computer technology that is capable of giving these students the practice and support they need is so important.

There are computer programs out there that are sold as a cure for dyslexia, but the research that I'm familiar with does not support the advantage of using programs that don't explicitly work on practicing reading.

Guinevere Eden, PhD, Past President, International Dyslexia Association

From the perspective of families, there is still a lot of confusion about what it is to have a dyslexic child, what the best path is, and how to travel it quickly. Parents don't have much time, and as years goes by, things become more problematic and more desperate. I think that the big breakthrough in the area of dyslexia is going to be in really having a better handle on our knowledge and making sure it translates across different disciplines so that what goes on in schools has a basis in neuroscience. We need to understand why certain interventions are effective, and use our knowledge from cognitive neuroscience to make them even more effective.

Eliza Milton
Churchill Center and School, St. Louis, Missouri

My worst public school experience was being pulled out my classroom for special ed. services. It made me feel excluded from my class and we only played games. But when teachers at Churchill met my individual needs, the small steps and strategies allowed me to reach my goals in reading and writing. I am an athlete, and hold multiple records in track. I also play on a traveling field hockey team.

Dyslexics,

What do you say?

Kim Bucciantini, Graduate of The Forman School

I'm a much better learner when I can be hands-on and see what I'm doing. I'm not a good out-of-the-book, lecture-learner. But I'm not disabled. I can learn as well as everyone else. It's just that it takes more effort and time.

Alyssa Bredin

Eric Steinberg, Parent and dyslexic

I came to terms with having dyslexia when I was about twenty years old and worked for a man for whom I had a huge amount of respect – very, very bright. Now, one of the ways dyslexia affects me is in spelling. I remember him saying to me, "You know, spelling is not a sign of intelligence; it's a skill. I, myself, am a horrible speller." At that moment it was okay for me, and from that point I started thinking of myself as maybe being an intelligent person.

I've become a master of using context to figure out what an unknown word is because I really don't have the ability to sound something out. If I read one of the Harry Potter books, for example, I literally have to make up a name for every one of the characters because I have no way of pronouncing their real names, so the way that I enjoy those sorts of books is by making up the names as I go.

I think that memorizing is a fundamental skill for people with dyslexia. Because you cannot pronounce certain words when you read them, you have a very keen sense of listening to what they sound like and repeating them when you hear them somewhere else, and so you memorize those words. Years ago, I heard about an interesting skill from a tutor, whose parlor trick to identify dyslexia was to ask a person to spell a word forward and backward. I realized I could do that too, because I visualize words as I have memorized them. Somebody who spells phonetically couldn't do that.

Elisha Wenzel
Hudson Valley Community College, Troy, New York

In high school, we had to work in groups and my teacher put me with a kid who said, "Oh great, I get the resource kid." I cried and felt ashamed and embarrassed. But I also worked hard to get into college. My most difficult experience in college is when I have to drop a class. I was too ashamed to ask for help at first, and at one point a professor suggested that I drop his course before it brought my GPA down. I was disappointed with myself, but from then on, I decided to ask for help when I needed it, even though that meant putting my pride aside. That's a small price to pay when the reward is a bright future.

Teachers,

What do you say?

Arlene Sonday, Founding Fellow and first President of the Academy of Orton

Research shows that children who are on top of phonological awareness have the best chance of learning to read later on. This is fairly clear.

Roger Saunders, Past President, International Dyslexia Association and helped found Jemicy School

We feel that children with dyslexia learn best with a multisensory approach. You teach the sound, but you reinforce it kinesthetically. When I work with children, adolescents, or even adults, I tell them, "Close your eyes, and write the letter in the air. Say the sound, and feel your muscles move." That reinforces the power of auditory and kinesthetic input. As a matter of fact, several times I've had children who said, "Oh no, Mr. Saunders, I've forgotten how to make an *m*," and I'd say, "Quickly, make it in the air!" And after that, they could write it on paper. I tell them that if they put it in that way, they can get it out again that way.

Margie Gillis, EdD, Senior Scientist, Haskins Laboratories

We try to help children start to be sensitive to the sound structure of language. We don't expect kids in pre-K to be able to hear all the sounds that kids in kindergarten hear, but we know that if we get them sensitive to sound and the rhythm of language, they are going to be set up to hear those sounds when they are developmentally ready.

Evelyn Russo is helping children develop an understanding of the alphabetic principle, which is that these sounds that come out of my mouth and make words connect with these arbitrary abstract symbols called letters. And in order to read, you have to be able to match the sounds coming out of your mouth to those letters and eventually, to those words. Just getting them to be able to take that first sound out of the word *seal* is difficult because it is not something that we are biologically wired to do. We have to be taught explicitly to become aware of that.

That foundational awareness and understanding is going to take kids faster, more easily, and more completely to reading success. We want to set kids up for reading automatically, without thinking about it, so the cognitive disk space can be used for comprehension, which is the whole point of reading. But in order for that to happen, they have to make those connections, and the sooner they make those connections, the better.

The Orton-Gillingham concept is based on fundamental principles of the structure of the English language. Language practitioner Samuel Orton, his wife, June Orton, and her colleague, Anna Gillingham, understood that some children could not learn to read without particular help in mastering the sound system of our very complex language. They teased the language apart and figured out how to do this methodically and sequentially, so that children could master every step. They put together a scope and sequence, systematized the sound structure of the English language, and established a framework so that teachers could translate it for students.

Children must understand the sound system, the phonology, which is complex in and of itself, but also must map that onto a complex writing system, an orthography. We have learned from Orton and Gillingham's wisdom and their work over many, many years that this method isn't just for children with dyslexia; this works well for all children. We owe it to all kids to teach them the sounds and structure of their language.

Arlene Sonday, Founding Fellow and first President of the Academy of Orton

The federal government has funded multimillion dollar studies, and they've all come out with the same basic result: phonics is really an important part of a reading program. They've never said that every child needs phonics to learn, but they do say that a study of phonics should be a part of a program because some children really do need it to learn to read and spell.

fusdaraded.

Alyssa Bredin

Years ago, we didn't know that spelling is a good predictor of reading comprehension, but we did see that children who could not read words automatically, with fluency, did not comprehend what they read. And we knew that if they could spell the word, they could read it because spelling comes after reading. These things made sense, and we did them because they worked, but we didn't have the background of research. Now, however, more and more people are reading the research and paying attention to it, and that's what is influencing some dramatic changes in educational programs.

Margie Gillis, EdD, Senior Scientist, Haskins Laboratories

It's true that individuals have differing strengths in learning styles, and for a while in education, we all jumped on the bandwagon of figuring out whether kids are visual learners, auditory learners, or kinesthetic learners, thinking that's how we'll teach them, and it will solve all the problems. But it is not so simple, and we have found that by and large, when we experience something and interact with it in multiple ways, that is how we are going to remember it. When you think back to when you were a kid, what do you remember when you were learning? It is usually something that was engaging, often involving your body. It was fun, and you felt successful at it. When you own it, you remember it.

Here is how we use the research to get from there to here. First, we study it. We spend a lot of time reading it, and it is not always written in laymen's language. We can go to someone like Ken Pugh who can explain it in terms that are more understandable.

We have round table seminars with colleagues, and together work on digesting the research and understanding it at a deep level. That way, we can make it real, and discuss ways to make it useable for teachers. *What are the implications for this in second grade reading instruction? What would this look like in the literacy center during reading group?* Our translation of the research into practical teaching applications really helps teachers understand both how and why to do something with their students.

We also have cross-talk that is really powerful. Haskins Literacy Specialists talk to the researchers, translate their work into applications for teachers, and then go back to the teachers and ask how it worked. *How did this go in your classroom? How did the kids respond? What did you notice happening?* We collect the data and bring it back to the researchers. *This is what we learned from this, but here's a question that keeps coming up. Let's see if we can design a study to explore it.* It takes a team of people to really think it through.

Diana Hanbury King, Founder of The Kildonan School

Since I first met Anna Gillingham, a lot has changed. We had a phonics books called *Eye and Ear, Book I and II*, and a little book of phonology called *Word Mastery*, and that was all. Everything else, we had to create ourselves. There are so many more materials available now, although in a way, it's a disadvantage because teachers tend to give a child a page in a workbook, rather than creating a match to precisely address the needs of that child.

Also, now there is more brain research, but it doesn't change what we do; it validates what we do. And beyond that, the fundamentals of our teaching, the necessity of making it multisensory, the step-by-step approach, going from the easiest to the more difficult, and the more common to the least common, all of that still holds true.

Nancy Cushen White, EdD, Associate Clinical Professor and Learning Disabilities Specialist

Parents want to help their children, and they want to believe that there is something they can do that will be fast. And that is the reason for the accrediting and certifying organizations that have grown in the last decade, such as the International Multisensory Structured Language Education Council and the Alliance for Accreditation and Certification under the umbrella of the International Dyslexia Association, so that the public can be protected from approaches that have no sound basis in research.

Even with an approach that is sound, there must be fidelity to its use. People must have more than a weekend or a few hours of training. They must have a background in not only the *how* and the *what* of a particular method but also the *why.* They need to have practiced the method, supervised by experts who can guide them. It isn't an easy route. It takes time.

Diana Hanbury King, Founder of The Kildonan School

In sports, many dyslexics have an enhanced sense of balance. Think of Greg Louganis, the Olympic diver, balanced on the edge of a diving platform. This is why we have horseback riding at Kildonan, and in the summer we have water skiing, and in the winter we have snow skiing. We are a small school, and again and again, we outperform schools that actually recruit for skiing. The sense of balance in many people with dyslexia is an advantage. It is not commonly mentioned, but it is a strength.

Arlene Sonday, Founding Fellow and first President of the Academy of Orton

Vocabulary and comprehension improve by reading more. If you read a book on skiing and read about all the ski paraphernalia and the

Scott Zangara

skiing moves and the snow, by the time you finish the book, you have a pretty good idea of all the terminology. You also learn to comprehend style by reading a variety of materials because essays are written differently than riddles, and riddles differently than newspaper articles, and newspaper articles differently than textbooks. Children with dyslexia who have not been offered appropriate intervention do not read a lot, so they are deprived of all this.

Margie Gillis, EdD, Senior Scientist, Haskins Laboratories

Districts spend a lot of money on materials and not enough on the professional development to get the teachers the information and understanding they need. At Haskins, we are firm believers that it is the teacher who teaches the children to read, not the reading program. And it takes a teacher who understands a lot about reading to take whatever reading program is coming down the pike and make it work effectively for kids.

It doesn't have to be expensive. We say, "Show us what you've got, and we'll help you make it better." We are not going to sell you the fancy-schmancy new program. We are not a program. We don't have any materials to sell. We are non-profit. We give teachers knowledge. Well, we don't give it away. We have to pay our mentors. But we translate the research for teachers so they can take what they have in their classrooms already and make it work better. We don't publish a how-to manual – we don't have a book. We keep learning new things, so a book would be out of date a month from now.

Dyslexia Advocates,

What do you say?

Marcia Henry, PhD, Past President, International Dyslexia Association

From the mid- to late-1800s, when public education was mandated, most children learned to read with McGuffey Readers, primers with a moralistic touch that were phonetically based. Later, children learned to read using stories with limited vocabularies, such as, *Sad Sam sat on a mat.* These stories weren't very interesting, but children continued to pick up the idea that letters corresponded with sounds. And so, early instruction was very phonetic.

But in the 1930s, a group of professors advised, *This is going too slowly, and children don't need to learn like that, so let's just have them memorize words.* If you learned to read using the whole word, or look-say method with Dick and Jane, you didn't learn that Jane started with a /j/ and that the *a* was a long vowel because of the silent *e.* You just saw a picture of a little blonde girl, and under it was a configuration of the symbols *J-a-n-e.* And you just memorized that that word represented the little girl, and that was fine. This look-say method worked well for children with good visual memory. It did not work for children who needed more information about the language: *What are the sounds?*

Rudolph Flesch wrote a bestselling book, *Why Johnny Can't Read,* in the 1950s. Flesch argued that Johnny can't read because he doesn't get any phonics instruction early on. And because of the simplistic stories, *Run, run, run. See Sally run!*, children were not developing an appreciation for literature. Some teachers swung back to phonics, but others stuck with the rote-memory technique.

In the 1980s and 1990s, the prevailing approach was called whole-language. Teachers read to children and guided them to figure out the words based on context, visual cues, and an understanding of the story structure. Now, there were lots of good things about whole language, including a heightened appreciation for fine children's literature, but for kids who didn't understand the phonetic system and had difficulty decoding, it was murder because no phonics were taught. These were not just children with dyslexia and not just English language learners who didn't have English as a primary language. These were also children who seemed ready to learn to read, but again, needed more information beyond context and memorization to be successful.

And now we are swinging back again on that pendulum for all sorts of reasons, but primarily because in the last twenty years, we've had funding to support a closer look at reading instruction and a movement to demand research-based reading instruction in our classrooms, instead of the next feel-good approach.

Peggy McCardle, PhD, National Institute for Child Health and Human Development (NICHD)

Kids learn to read through high-quality instruction that includes the major components of reading: phonemic awareness, phonics, fluency, vocabulary, and reading comprehension. When I talk about decoding, I lump together phonemic awareness and phonics. When you have really good decoding skills, when you can read well, you probably don't need any more instruction in that area across your education and as an adult. However, you are always going to be learning vocabulary. Once you've mastered fluency, you've got it, but if I pick up a text on nuclear physics and try to read it out loud to you, I'm not going to be very fluent without some practice. I'm going to stumble over some words that I'm not used to, and when I stumble over a great big word that is not in my vocabulary, I'm going to fall back to decoding.

I think that some work on morphology, on how you pull apart words to look for roots in prefixes or suffixes, and how you tear a word apart not only to pronounce it, but also to figure out its meaning, is a sort of *decoding plus*. Louisa Moats talks a lot about this when she works with teachers on the structure of the English language and how decoding, vocabulary, and fluency mesh and affect comprehension. Reading comprehension begins from the time a child starts to read, but it gets a lot more complex in the upper grades.

Marcia Henry, PhD, Past President, International Dyslexia Association

Dr. Samuel Orton was a Renaissance man with medical degrees in both psychiatry, neuropathology, and a reading degree from Harvard. He was interested in learning from people with various disorders and brain differences that he felt were biologically based.

One of his positions was Director of Psychiatry at the medical school at the University of Iowa. To serve the rural community, he set up a mobile health unit to look at children and adults who were having learning problems, along with difficulties in memory and attention.

He became fascinated with a sixteen-year-old boy who had a fantastic mind for understanding mechanical things. Dr. Orton showed him a tractor that could plow and do all sorts of things. Then after he took it away, the boy could explain exactly how each process worked. But when asked to read a second-grade passage, he couldn't read a word. When asked to copy the passage, he copied it perfectly. When asked to spell words from the same passage, he couldn't do it. Dr. Orton said, "This is obviously a bright person. He has all these wonderful abilities: copying, visualizing, analyzing, and yet he can't read and write at a second-grade level." And that just whetted Dr. Orton's appetite for learning more about reading.

He collected a group of specialists, and set up a practice in New York. He met Anna Gillingham in the early 1930s. A psychologist at New York's Ethical Culture School, she asked to study with him after she struggled to help some very bright children who happened also to have problems with reading. Another teacher there, Bessie Stillman, also embraced Dr. Orton's ideas of teaching with a multisensory approach, saying, "We can't just depend on the visual pathway. We have to think of the auditory pathway and the kinesthetic-tactile. How does it feel to make the sound /m/versus /n/? How does it feel to write an *m* versus an *n*? "

They sought connections between sensory input and the brain: how it feels to hear sounds, to see the letters that make the sounds, to use muscles to form the letters that make the sounds, to put all the parts together in words and meanings, and ultimately, to use this multisensory information to read and write fluently.

Bessie Stillman and Anna Gillingham started writing manuals and developing lesson plans. And in a way, the actual methodology should probably be called Orton-Gillingham-Stillman. But in 1966, long after Dr. Orton had died, Mrs. Orton, who had continued his practice, wrote a chapter in a very important book called *Developmental Dyslexia*. She coined the term *Orton-Gillingham approach*, and that's what she called her chapter. And that term stuck.

With this approach, children learn about letter sounds, syllables, word parts, and meaning parts, which are called morphemes: prefixes, suffixes, Latin roots, and so on. They learn strategies for decoding, for spelling, and for enhancing their vocabularies. They don't have to rely on memorization, and they are not overburdening one learning pathway because they receive input through multiple pathways. For most dyslexics, this kind of multisensory instruction is successful and effective.

Devin DiPiazza
Spring Valley School, Birmingham, Alabama

I used to be so disorganized, disruptive to others, and felt low of myself. I felt so different when I had a B on my paper and almost ALL the wrong answers were overlooked. That's the most ashamed and unaccepted I've ever felt. Spring Valley has given me the ability to believe in myself. I now understand that I only learn in a different way, a unique way, and it's not a disability but a GIFT! I worked hard to become a better soccer player. When I was team captain, our soccer team went undefeated for the season.

9
How Is Dyslexia an Advantage?

I figured out that if I accepted my disability and worked with my strengths, I really could succeed.
Luke Bornheimer

Harvey,

What do you say?

One child at a time, people are making a difference. One by one. Pebble in the pond. Little by little, more teachers are effectively teaching more dyslexics, and this is the focus of our film: bringing awareness to policy makers, parents, and educators to enable them to make informed decisions.

With the technology of the fMRI, scientists can see how the brain functions. During my scanning procedure, I was given the tall-letter task. I had to press a certain button if a letter was tall or short. The images produced showed how much blood was rushing around inside my brain when I looked at certain things and thought about them. Results on this test show that dyslexics (not just me) recognize tall and short letters a few hundredths of a second slower than normal people, or as I should say, people with normality.

Another study uses impossible figures, images that resemble Escher-type drawings that are flashed in front of a person being tested in an fMRI. The person has to decide whether the figure could really exist or not. This study hasn't been finished, although it might be done by the time our book and movie are. Early data indicate that dyslexics recognize if the figures are possible or impossible a little bit faster than the average Joe.

I'm just a simple country filmmaker, so don't take my word for it, but what this may point to is that dyslexics may think better with images, not letters. And back in the day, these picture thinkers may have been wired this way to be highly skilled at reading clouds (important for sailors), or reading water (important for fishermen), or tracking animals in jungles (important for hunters). And what this may imply is that dyslexia has remained through our genetic history because it brings with it a crucial survival skill.

Here we are again at the notion that we should appreciate all types of different minds, and we actually need them all without *curing* any of them, to keep going in this world.

When I was younger, I ended up working with horses and then moving on to dealing with people. By working with animals, I gained skills in how to read people. I believe I can read a person and predict what they will do next just about a nanosecond before they do it, and I learned this through working with animals. Overall, I believe I have a very high social IQ.

Desi Gialanella
The Gow School, South Wales, New York

Jose, Desi, and Izer

Once at school, I had to sit on a chair in the hall the entire day because I couldn't do my work. I told the teachers that I didn't understand it, but they thought that I just wasn't trying. At the Gow School, I like the small classes because the teachers pay more attention to me. I have gotten better at reading, writing, math, everything. I love art and making things with my hands. I am also a magician. I can amaze my friends with card tricks and optical illusions. Science is my favorite subject and I can climb just about anything!

Brain Specialists,
What do you say?

Jeffrey Gilger, PhD, Associate Dean, Purdue University

We call someone who has dyslexia and particular gifts a twice-exceptional person. These kids are often not identified in elementary school because they have other strong skills that allow them to hide their reading difficulties. Sometimes they don't get identified until late in high school or in college. The sad part is that by then, they carry a lot of emotional baggage from the stress of hiding a part of themselves. And because their special talent hasn't been recognized, it can be too late for it to develop as it might have. It is important to not just remediate the reading difficulty, but also to build on the talent, and to teach people to develop and use their talent, not only to help them get along with reading problems, but to make wonderful lives for themselves. Not everyone has to be a good reader to be successful.

The idea persists that some people with dyslexia may have special abilities in nonverbal areas that people without dyslexia do not have: holistic, visual, spatial, mapping, and creative skills. And that myth has been around for a long time. I call it a myth because there is no empirical data at this point, although research is ongoing, and there have been lots of anecdotal evidence and stories to support this.

I've been doing some work with people who have both dyslexia and particular nonverbal talents. These are people who do not read well, but have normal intelligence. However, when it comes to measuring their visual intelligence, they are off the charts, higher than 98 percent of the people in the population. We've done some brain scans, and these brains don't look like dyslexic brains, but they don't look like typical brains either. They look like a combination of dyslexia plus something else. And that something else seems to be the stuff that is loaded up in the parietal area of the brain, the part that specializes in holistic, visual skills like 3-D rotation, and certain types of mental math processing skills.

When we think about brilliant people in the nonverbal domain, Einstein comes to mind. When he died, there was an autopsy study of his brain. If you were to look at Einstein's brain, you would think that it looked pretty much like a normal brain, but a couple of things would stand out. Every brain has the folds and bumps that we picture when we think of a brain, but Einstein's had some unique gyral morphologies. In particular he had more cortex, a thicker layer of cells in the parietal area, particularly on the right hemisphere but also on the left hemisphere, and he had a fissure that went all the way over the top of his head. Most people don't have this. Einstein may have been dyslexic. He certainly was brilliant nonverbally. I think he is a good example of how differences in brain structure and differences in how the brain works can provide both disabilities and gifts.

When I teach classes, I suggest that students walk down the street and picture people as being nothing more than little stick figures with huge brains, and to realize that in all the people they are passing, all their personalities, all their cognitive abilities, all this is in their brains. That's all we are, brains that weigh two or three pounds. But in a population, we have a whole distribution of these brains with differences in structures and functions and therefore, differences in behaviors. The idea of a normal brain is hypothetical. There is no such thing as a normal brain, but most of us hover around a hypothetical norm. Everybody has a little bit of this that's above average and a little bit of that that's below average. Our brains came about because of development, and much of it, but not all of it, happened in the uterus. So some development is regulated by genes, and some is regulated by environment.

There are some data that indicate that people can lose the ability to think nonverbally. Einstein even talked about this. The older he got, and the more he was expected to be a teacher and put his thoughts into writing to explain his thinking, the more frustrating and difficult he found it to think creatively in a nonverbal mode, beyond words. So, if you take a five-year-old and drill him in phonics, maybe you can get him up to an average performance in reading. But when you are treating that part of his brain, you are also treating his whole brain. You can't have an isolated intervention that doesn't affect everything the kid is perceiving and thinking about and feeling. You treat the whole brain. So now, he can read, but he might have lost his gift.

Pop Quiz #6

By routinely applying to the classroom the lessons learned from scientific findings, most reading failure could be avoided. It is estimated that the current failure rate of 20–30 percent could be reduced to the range of_____.

     a. 15–18 percent

     b. 10–15 percent

     c. 2–10 percent

     d. It is not possible to reduce the current failure rate.

(Answer at the back of the book)

How Is Dyslexia an Advantage?

Gordon Sherman, PhD, Executive Director of Newgrange School and Education Center

It is all about what the culture wants from your brain. If you can't deliver, and the culture really needs this from you, like reading in our culture, or like singing in another culture, you can be labeled as having a learning disability. But it is not so much that you are disabled, it is that the environment disables you. However, the environment changes all the time, and in thirty years, who knows who is going to be in the next group that is labeled that way?

That is why the fight that we're fighting in terms of dyslexia is going to apply to all those groups as we move along in the future. In the same way that the environment can disable somebody, we can control the environment and make it a lot less of a traumatic experience.

If music ability is the important element in society, and if a person lacks musical talent, but we identify that problem early, intervene early, and teach music in a different way – maybe not in a linear way with note after note after note, but using some of the modern computer methods for composing music – then we might see a very different type of brain, even though that brain didn't have a genetic advantage in music. We can change the whole scenario by intervening early and teaching directly in an appropriate way, using what that brain does really well.

The outer part of the cortex does not contain any nerve cell bodies in most cases because there is a membrane in the brain that stops neurons from going too far as they migrate to the cortex, except in dyslexia where neurons do migrate into that outer layer. This hasn't received a lot of attention lately. It was groundbreaking work back in the early '80s, showing that there is a biological effect in dyslexia. Geschwind had something to say about this too, that we must consider another paradoxical possibility that minor malformations like these may often be associated not with abnormal function, but with distinctly superior capacities in certain areas such as visual-spatial processing.

These ectopias, or abnormally positioned neurons, occur mostly in the language areas of the brain, particularly on the left side. And they are connected differently. How do you change the way the brain is processing information? You change the connections of the brain. So we now know there's a gene that plays a role in dyslexia that affects the developing cortex, and these ectopias are an example of modulated neuronal migration right smack dab in the verbal working memory area, which may relate to the particular difficulty with verbal working memory that many people with dyslexia experience.

As Norman Geschwind asked, *What if we could prevent these brain changes and thus prevent the appearance of dyslexia?* I think that would be a disaster. It certainly would limit cerebrodiversity. Might we find that we have deprived society of an irreplaceable group of individuals endowed with remarkable talent?

Ken Pugh: Gordon and some others have done work suggesting that while children with dyslexia have a harder time with print, under some conditions, they actually seem to perform even better than nondyslexic children when doing visual-spatial processing of figures.

The data are intriguing, and we're getting very excited about some of these initial brain activation maps; they're showing discrimination between the brain systems for reading and the brain systems for figural and visual-spatial processing.

Gordon: If this turns out to be the case, this study will change the landscape for dyslexia. It will change our understanding of what is really going on in the brains of people with dyslexia, and it could transform the way we go about teaching them. This study begins to look at these kids as the rich and complex human beings that they really are.

Ken: There is a long, anecdotal history that suggests that many people who are particularly good at visual-spatial processing tend to be poor readers. Consider people in engineering, in art, in architecture, in medicine, in neuroradiology (who have to look at three-dimensional representations of the brain and figure out what's going on). Again, it's not hard science, but there is certainly anecdotal history.

We see many areas in the brain that are responding vigorously to images of geometric patterns, but we don't see areas that are responding with more intensity to reading, so it's a very striking difference. One could hypothesize that the problem with reading might be a by-product of having such a strongly visual-spatial brain.

Gordon: Or we might see the visual-spatial ability as a strength that does not have great value at school, and the indirect result is that a child who does not have equal strength as a reader is devalued. Dyslexic brains have a much different set of experiences than reading brains, and that is something that still has to be untangled.

Ken: I am particularly moved by Gordon's notion of cerebrodiversity and how we need to see dyslexia not as a biomedical condition, but as a different blueprint for building a brain. Understanding dyslexia in terms of strengths really makes sense. If you're around people with dyslexia, you know that they do not have disabled brains.

Gordon: The environment takes the difference in their brains and turns it into a disability. Our general understanding of dyslexia is that dyslexic people do certain things very well. This moves the focus from disability and problem to strength and teaching to the strengths.

Gordon Sherman, PhD, Executive Director of Newgrange School and Education Center

So, here are three critical questions: Are certain talents related to dyslexia? Do visual-spatial processing abilities increase the chance of developing reading disabilities? And is there a basic incompatibility between visual-spatial processing and language processing?

What is talent, anyway? It is a match between biology, brain processing, and the environment. You need to have some kind of good sensory input, even if it is just from one sense. You need to do basic computations of that sensory input. You need a decent memory, you need to be able to do a complex and creative analysis, and you need to have some kind of motor output, although you could dispute that. You could be talented and not have any means for or interest in output, but then you're the only one who knows that you're talented. You need to be motivated, and you need to be really courageous as well, especially as a student, as a child. To stand out from other students, even if it's for a good reason, is very courageous.

What is visual-spatial processing? It's the ability to locate points in three-dimensional space: perceiving depth; orienting lines in space; understanding geometric relationships; forms and shapes; tracking movements; moving an object over time (which is an incredibly complex thing to do - our brains do it well - computers don't); rotating an object; global navigation; and reading a map. I would suggest that most people with dyslexia have a strong visual-spatial channel.

Talents may be hidden because it's difficult for students to come to the realization that they could have a disability as well as a talent. And many times those talents or strengths are just put off to the side, *Oh yeah, I can do that kind of thing, but I can't read. And that's really who I am.* We know that chronic stress affects brain processing and brain ability, and I can't think of any group of people that goes through more stress than children with dyslexia, spending day after day in a classroom environment that is not designed for them. Even if a talent may be there, it's often disguised.

We've all seen a list of prominent people with dyslexia who actually have been tested in some form. It contains movie producers and actors. Robert Rauschenberg, the artist. Paul Orfalea, who started Kinko's. David Boies, the trial attorney. Whoopi Goldberg. Adam Viniteri, field goal kicker for the New England Patriots. Tommy Hilfiger, the fashion designer. Jerry Pinkney, the Caldecott Medal-winning illustrator. Reyn Guyer, who came up with the quintessential dyslexic invention, the Nerf football. Mick Fleetwood, the drummer. Henry Winkler. Jay Leno. Cher. Bruce Jenner, the decathlon gold medal winner. Greg Louganis, the diving champion. Jim Shea, who took a skeleton sled down a mountain and won a gold medal. Dyslexia runs in families, and so did gold medals in his case. His father won a gold medal, and so did his grandfather. I wonder if they were all interesting in terms of the way they processed information. I suppose that goes without saying if you go down mountains like that.

In 2002, *Fortune* magazine identified a number of dyslexic CEOs, including Charles Schwab, Richard Branson of Virgin Airlines, Craig McCaw, a pioneer in the cellular industry, and John Chambers of Cisco.

Geschwind believed that talent accompanies dyslexia and wrote a lot about that. This is one of his quotes: "Making talented brains is not simple. Nature has probably adopted many (strategies) for the achievement of this end. It is indeed quite possible that dyslexia may be an unwanted byproduct of a mechanism that evolved as a means of increasing the numbers of certain types of high talent."

There are a number of quotes that keep me up at night. Here is another from Emerson Pugh: "If the human brain were so simple that we could understand it, we would be so simple that we couldn't."

Dyslexics,

What do you say?

Austen Marshall

Tom West, Author

We're burrowing deeper and deeper into the pathology of dyslexia, looking only at the things people with dyslexia are not good at, and looking only at the things that are wrong with the dyslexic brain. We've had almost no experience with what is going right with these brains. The talent side of dyslexia should be studied, and it is about time we started.

Luke Bornheimer, Graduate of The Forman School

I have the ability to brainstorm. I can come up with ideas and force myself beyond thinking, *Oh, that's not going to work!* I have the ability to not give up and to keep trying to come up with other ways to solve something. The Forman School has helped me with that, giving me the freedom to think and not feel restricted in speaking out. I can throw out a couple of ideas, and I've gotten to the point where if someone says, "No, that's not a good idea," I'll go right on to the next one. I'm not sitting there thinking, *Oh man, that was such a bad idea.* I just say, *Okay, that's fine. It probably wasn't such a good idea. Let's go on to the next one and try to find something new and better that will work.*

After my first year here, I figured out that if I accepted my disability and worked with my strengths, I really could succeed. I think that helped me feel free to share my thoughts and feelings on different issues.

Zach Capriotti, Inmate at State Correctional Institution

Because I couldn't read, I would get information using my photographic memory. I remember how to get everywhere. I can go from Lebanon, Pennsylvania to New York City, to Harrisburg, or to Pittsburgh without knowing any streets. I just know how to get there by memory.

My prison sentence motivated me to start reading and writing. You can pay attorneys all the money you want, but they really will not fight

for you. You must fight for yourself in order to prove any innocence. And I do not want my son to grow up without me, so I learned how to read so I could study the law books and fight my own case. I think it is going pretty well right now. Once I understood that it was very important for me to understand the legal words and what was in the paragraphs, things got much better for

Andrea Shaw

me. I had to understand in order to fight my case.

I would like to teach my son how to read. I would like to read him *The Chronicles of Narnia.* I like that series by C. S. Lewis: *The Lion, the Witch and the Wardrobe, The Puppet Master, The Silver Chair,* and *Prince Caspian.*

Olivia Hanson, Graduate of The Forman School

When people put me down and say I can't do anything, I think, *I'm going to prove them wrong and do something really difficult that I am passionate about.* I show them, and I guess I show myself as well.

When it comes to acting, I can put myself into a character and make it seem realistic. Sometimes I'll have to pause and try to figure out how to read a line. I'll explain that I have a few questions about some of the words, but it doesn't affect anything. It doesn't mean I'm not perfect for the part.

Jack Horner, Paleontologist

I never met Michael Crichton until we were in the limo together on the way to *Jurassic Park* for the premiere, but he based his Alan Grant character in his book on a combination of me and another fellow who lives around here. One day I was sitting at home, and a guy named Steven Spielberg called me up and asked me if I wanted to work on a movie. I said yes, and that's all there was to that.

I always wanted to be a paleontologist, and I figured that I could be one no matter what. I found my first dinosaur bone when I was eight. My father and mother would actually give me rides to look for dinosaur bones. I excavated my first dinosaur skeleton when I was in high school. Even if I had to work at some other job, this would have to be my hobby. I don't do anything else. That's all I do, paleontology. I love it. But reading is the very hardest thing I do in my life, and that's why I say it is overrated.

Keaghan Hamilton, Graduate of The Forman School

For the most part, having dyslexia has made me a stronger person. I'm not afraid to say what I think or be told that it's the wrong answer because there are only so many things that have either a right or wrong answer. I may not be book-smart, but I can be smart in other ways. It is always a challenge, and I am always in competition with myself. People say, "You can't do this," and I want to prove them wrong. I don't give up. I was told I wouldn't go to a good college, but I've already been accepted at some pretty good ones.

Cary Spier, Parent of Sarah Spier, dyslexic, and documentary filmmaker

You don't have to be perfect at everything. How boring to be perfect. Dyslexic people are creative. For some reason, that side of their brain is on fire. I can do a film without ever writing a script. I see the entire film completed in my head. I see one, big, whole picture, and I think that's something dyslexics are very good at.

I think that dyslexics have an amazing sense of courage to walk in a classroom, or any environment, every single day, and not understand something and feel different. To do it day in and day out, and go home, cry, and be depressed, and then get up, put the boots back on, and go back into that environment, it's courageous.

Sarah Spier, Founder and President of Mwambao Alliance, Mwambao Primary School, Tanzania

Let's get the teachers to respect what we can do, so we're not sitting there like deer in the headlights. Let us show everybody else that we're not dumb. There are so many interesting people out there. Why aren't there interesting ways to teach us?

Dennis Miller
Riverside School, Richmond, Virginia

My worst experience in school was a bully that made fun of my poor reading skills. But at Riverside, I have made 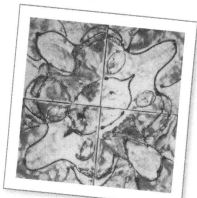 friends and am successful in school. I was voted Best All-Around Student. Expressing myself in art helped me achieve this.

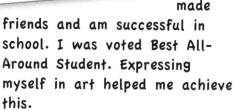

Aaron McLane, Special Effects Artist

I work in L.A. doing special effects. I love doing blood and guts, monster makeup, all the scary stuff. If dyslexia has affected me in my work, it would be when you have to be precise with your measurements. I'm trying to read something and do math on one side of my brain, and read something and think creatively on the other side. I can use my creativity to find different ways to look at something, and I am very outside of the box in that sense.

Stephen J. Cannell, Writer, Producer

As a young kid, if someone had said to me, "We can fix your academic trouble." I would have opted for it. I would have said, "Fix it! Fix it, please!" But now, with the perspective of age and having had my career, I realize that the way I think stems from having this condition. It has allowed me to do so much. I've had fun with it. You know, I wouldn't want it fixed.

Malcolm Alexander, Sculptor

Bradley Morell

I have the ability to retain things visually. When I did pieces for some of the major NFL teams, all I had to do was watch an athlete once, and I could get him down. I remember Joe Namath hunched back when he faded back to pass. I see and remember mannerisms. No one walks in the same way, and no one passes in the same way. Danny Lawson was a low passer.

Now with reading, word by word, backing up again and again, by the time I get to the end of the sentence, I can't remember how it began. But I've got that visual-spatial skill. I see the whole picture. I never sketch anything. I have made major monuments without a sketch.

Billy Blanks, Inventor of Tae Bo exercise program, fitness guru

I found out at thirty-five years old that it was dyslexia that hindered me from doing better at school. But I wouldn't say that dyslexia hindered me from being where I am in life, so I wouldn't want to go back and change my life. I've been in twenty-eight movies and ten TV shows. In order for me to prepare for a movie, my wife would read the script to me. As she read, I would memorize not just my part but everybody else's, too. I could quote the whole script. Knowing the other actors' parts helped me do a better job on mine. I was always good at memorizing, and I think that if I could have had somebody do that for me in school, I could have learned better. There are other ways to get what we need out of a class. It's not just books we need to read.

Joe Pantoliano, Emmy Award-winning actor

I think dyslexia is an asset. It's a great gift because we're tenacious. We have an ability to maintain and regulate and do three things at once. People think we're not paying attention, but it's almost like we've got to do that in order to comprehend better. If you ask me to concentrate, "Now, listen to me, Joey. Listen carefully to what I've got to tell you," I'm not going to get it. But if I'm listening to you and two other conversations, I'm there. I don't know how, but I am.

Sarah Joy Brown, Emmy Award-winning actress

I am able to concentrate on several things at once. I could listen to the teacher give a lecture, have a daydream which might or might not involve what she was talking about in the lecture, and still follow along with whatever was going on in the class. I don't know how, but my brain remembers what it hears. Everything.

When I started on *General Hospital,* I could memorize sixty pages in six minutes, no problem, as long as I could hear it out loud. Once I began acting in a soap opera, I realized that I have a gift for memorization. It took me a couple of years to realize that this is because my brain makes pictures of everything. Stories, music. Anything I've ever seen before. Anything I've heard. And dialogue is a lot like music. If you tell me a story, I see every detail. I see the color green of your grandmother's socks, and I can't possibly forget it. In school, when I would listen to lectures in class, I would associate the information with daydreams and pictures of my own life. Although I did not do the reading, I would ask my friends about the chapter and listen to them read their reports, and I would remember enough to feel like I was there. My daydreams were so vivid that they became a visual link to the information. That was one way that I learned to compensate.

Catherine Lusius

But it wasn't like I couldn't read. I want to make that clear. I could read. I just couldn't read books. I would rather pull my teeth out. Get hit by a bus. Reading a whole book made me nervous and dizzy. Everything moved. The colors changed. I would look at one and want to throw up. So I thought, *Well, I just prefer pictures and things that are auditory. That's just how I am.* But on tests, I never forgot anything I heard, and when I got into acting, I realized how beneficial this was.

I know now that dyslexia isn't a disability unless I choose to look at it that way. I may not be able to spell the word *friend* correctly – it just doesn't come to me – but I'm fine as long as I memorize things. That can be a challenge in an audition when you have to read from the script, acting as you go, but making it clear that you're not performing – you're reading. I can't do that. It doesn't come naturally to me. Even having the paper script in my hands makes me nervous. Suddenly I feel as if I'm in school, not in my creative element. And they don't go together. What does come naturally to me is acting. So I just memorize the lines, and if they don't hire me, then they don't. That's still better than trying to read off a page and looking like a complete idiot. So dyslexia can be a struggle, but I don't see it as a disability anymore.

Tom West, Author

I have been really interested in dyslexia because I come from a family of dyslexics. I had problems myself which were revisited when our boys were having difficulties. I can even look back and see it in my artist father. I didn't just want to fix our problems, though. I wanted to understand them in a larger way. I have wondered about the advantages of particular talents since I was a small child, and at a certain point, I got serious about it and started doing library research and looking at famous people who had a series of traits.

I'm not hung up on strict definitions of dyslexia. Researchers and scientists have to be, but my point of view is more historical. I looked at over one hundred years of different definitions, different times, and different understandings. I looked at lists of traits from neurologists, and then applied them to primary sources, letters, diary entries, and what friends and family and coworkers said about these people. I was particularly interested in finding highly visual abilities coupled with language difficulties of various kinds.

It used to be that literary skills were terribly important, high-level work, but I believe there's a new kind of literacy that relates to new technologies, where the rules of the game are different. Instead of someone who memorizes an algebraic equation, we need someone who can look at a computer visualization of enormously complex information, see a pattern change, and infer that something is happening in nature, or something is happening in a financial market.

I work a lot with computer graphic artists, and I feel as though I'm working with a sort of race of human beings who are leading the way for all the rest of the world, but nobody knows it yet except this tiny group. The rules are different for them because they have to be able to do something well that people in a conventional educational system haven't a clue how to do. I would argue that if we're all going to have to work at high levels of proficiency, one of the areas we have to be very proficient in is being able to interpret complex visual information. This takes a different type of brain.

Some business people can anticipate things. Some athletes always seem to be where the ball is going to be because they can model in their minds what's going to happen and speed it up. This is an extension of that visual-spatial capacity, but how on earth do we measure these things? I think that with new technologies, we can work out ways of measuring, but it will require new tools. The old pencil and paper and rotations in your mind will be inadequate.

I hear people say, "Oh, you're not thinking clearly unless you're thinking in words." But these are usually very verbal people who are not visual in their thinking. A really spectacularly innovative thinker, Einstein, described how his most important work was created by playing with images in his head, and how difficult it was to convert those images into words and numbers that could be understood by others. But new technologies sidestep the need to convert the results of visual processing into words. We can take a visual idea and manipulate it and present it on a computer screen, so that the content is created and received without ever having to leave the visual realm. Our culture has been tied to an old technology of text and books, but this new technology is going to change the rules of the game.

Sarah Joy Brown, Emmy Award-winning actress

One of my hobbies is film editing. The dyslexic in me is fascinated watching moving images and splicing them together to tell a story. That's the way that I think. When I watch an edit, I can tell instantly if there's a black frame. Where others may not see it, it pops right out for me. That's another positive, and someday, it may make me a great director and a great editor.

Damali Archie
Triad Academy, Winston-Salem, North Carolina

At my old school, class was always going too fast. I felt alone and disconnected. I tried to fit in but it didn't work. I had to ask other students for help and it made me feel embarrassed. They would call me retarded because I was not a good reader. But I'm smart! My reading is getting better. In my LT class at Triad, I read a story fluently and could understand it. It made me feel good because I overcame something I thought I would never be able to do. I'm getting better and better with practice. I also love planning intricate designs and making jewelry.

Tom West, Author

The brain is different in dyslexic people – we know that from the neurologists. In simplest terms, you have a lot of difficulties with the language that other people don't have. But you have visual-spatial abilities with right-hemisphere kinds of traits that can lead to great success in science: being able to imagine the movement of molecules or to imagine what it's like to be on a light beam. You have a wonderful imagination that lets you do things that other people cannot do. But it's a trade-off. Yeats is a wonderful poet in terms of conjuring up images and ideas through metaphors, but at the same time, as one editor would say, he would make astonishing spelling errors. That part of his brain didn't work very well, and that is what has fascinated me for many years.

In these primary sources, the original letters and diaries, I could see quite clearly a pattern of core traits of dyslexia that come from neurologists' definition of the condition: late use of language, inability to learn to read, poor language skills, poor sight reading, and poor oral reading. There is a list of ninety-some traits. I also look for a set of positive traits such as high visual proficiency, mechanical skill, global thinking, and that old cliché, thinking outside the box. Those are also on my long list.

Robbie Tonner

The neurologist Norman Geschwind thought of dyslexia as evidence of nature's way of producing different kinds of brains. If you have a vanilla kind of brain, you can do lots of things easily but all in the middling area. To have an extreme talent in one area, you have to sacrifice talent in another. Geschwind said that it's a survival mechanism of the human race to have people with dyslexia be able to do things that the human race never knew it needed to be able to do.

This is another part that fascinates me: dyslexics who are successful are often way out ahead of everybody else, and the teachers and the testers haven't a clue as to what they are talking about. Albert Einstein is a wonderful example of that. Very few people understood the kind of thing he was thinking about in 1903, but as he talked about his various theories of relativity, there were a few more people who began to understand, and now, in the field of telecommunications and satellites, these ideas are conventions of engineering, understood and used every day. It took us nearly a hundred years to catch up to what Albert Einstein was doing in his imagination.

Many people with dyslexia are very visual in the way they work and the way they think. They may deal with words, like Yeats, but they're working from images, seeing things in their minds, and they may write, or draw a picture or create computer graphics based on these visual ideas. Yeats couldn't learn the alphabet when he was a little boy, and even though he became a very successful poet, he couldn't read his own poetry aloud without stumbling because of the word-finding and sight-reading problems that dyslexics typically have.

I argue that the printing press is the machine that created serious problems for dyslexics. In a culture of books, they had to read, and by definition, that's the problem they have. But computer graphics and supercomputing changed the game again because technology plays to the strengths of people with dyslexia rather than to their weaknesses.

If your memory is wired for the sound of the word rather than for the spelling of the word, your memory is going to be phonemic rather than lexical, and the spelling of the word will be secondary no matter how much remediation you have. Yeats writes that one time his father got so frustrated trying to teach him to read that he threw a book at his head.

I found misspellings in General George Patton's letters and an absence of periods at the ends of sentences. When Patton went to military school, he couldn't read certain types of text, and people thought he was being oppositional. He received military punishments because he could not read the hazing pledge out loud. His father wrote him back, saying, "You have to figure out how to read different kinds of typefaces. And you misspelled the word hazing. You drop the *e* and add *-ing*."

But when he did read, he read all sorts of military history and became a great scholar. Dyslexics may have trouble learning to read and trouble reading throughout their lives, but it doesn't stop them from doing it. If they are passionately interested in a subject, they can become wonderful scholars and poets. Dyslexia is an impediment, and people have to do extra work that people without dyslexia don't have to do, but passion for a topic drives them to find a way to get the information they need.

I believe that the technological world is changing again, and the most important tools are no longer books, but the new computer graphic tools that take information on any subject and convert it into a big moving picture. Complex information about complex things can be presented in complex multidimensional images, and certain brains will see and understand patterns, whether about science, financial markets, or anything else. Of course, that's the trick: to go without words, straight to the pattern, and most people with dyslexia can do that. But most teachers don't have a clue about this because it is out in front of what everybody else is able to do.

Delos Smith, Senior Economist for the Security Executive Council

It is common to use the words *learning disabilities* when speaking of students who struggle. But they apply to everyone. Everyone has weaknesses, so everyone must have some disabilities.

Society is full of labels, and they are so often negative. I think we should reverse the negative stigma that comes with the label of dyslexia, and focus on the positive advantages of having this condition. In many ways, it is a plus-something, rather than a disability. There are so many kinds of intelligences and talents. Of course we are different. Be proud to be different.

Pop Quiz #7

Learning disorders tend to run in families. The prognosis is generally good, however, for individuals whose dyslexia is:

a. identified early if they have a supportive family and friends and a strong self-image and are involved in a proper remediation program.

b. identified by sixth to eighth grade if they eat a well balanced breakfast and go to school most days.

c. ignored if they are told daily to "do your best."

d. none of the above. There is no hope for dyslexics.

(Answer at the back of the book)

Brendan Buckley
The Gow School, South Wales, New York

In third grade we were supposed to sit at the desk with our name on it. I couldn't find mine because I didn't know which one was my name. But at Gow I see how well I can do. Art is a creative outlet for me, and three of my pieces were chosen for the

Albright-Knox Art Gallery's Future Curators Teen Exhibition. I also take art classes and spend summers working in an art studio.

Parents,

What do you say?

Voncille Wright, Parent of Jo'Von Wright

Jo'Von has a sense of direction that is uncanny. When she and my niece are in New York City, it is Jo'Von who finds their way back to the train station. She really observes the environment, noticing things others don't even see. Then she takes it in, processes it, and determines which way to go. She uses her brain in a totally different way to solve her problems.

Jo'Von has learned a lot of life lessons as a result of her learning difference. She's learned that she has to work a little harder, and has developed a good work ethic. Although you can't tell it by her room, she is very organized when it comes to her learning and understands the importance of being prepared. Having a learning difference has taught her to be persistent and persevere where a lot of children her age would have given up. And she has learned to advocate, not only for herself, but for others. She has this banner of justice that she wears across her chest, and I think that's a result of the challenges she has faced.

We went to a conference in New York, and when we were leaving, Jo'Von said, "You know what, Mom? I feel good about being dyslexic." She saw so many bright people who spoke positively about their learning differences. Being around other people who are dyslexic and seeing the amazing things they can do has helped her understand better what she can do. Jo'Von has so many skills and so many abilities. How can we say that this child is disabled?

Marken P. Aboitiz
The Kildonan School, Amenia, New York

In my previous school, I was being exempted from the work my classmates were doing. At The Kildonan School, however, my teachers have respect for my preparation for college. I enjoy using film and photography to inspire others.

Teachers,

What do you say?

Diana Hanbury King, Founder of The Kildonan School

Brenda Sladen, a friend of mine who is a geneticist, thought about the condition of color blindness, or red-green insensitivity, for a long time, and questioned how it could be an advantage. Then she discovered that in World War II, men who were needed to fly reconnaissance planes were deliberately chosen for their color blindness because with red-green insensitivity, they were not fooled by camouflage. So, to primitive men who were color blind, they would not have been fooled by camouflage and would have seen that the dapple shade was really a giraffe that they were hunting. They would have been particularly keen-eyed hunters, observant of things that other people would not be able to notice.

Brenda Sladen theorizes that dyslexia has also carried an advantage since a time when people were living in caves, and that's how it became embedded as a human hereditary pattern. The dyslexic individuals in a primitive tribe of cavemen would have a better chance of survival because they would have particular skill in tracking, observing, and capturing animals, or knowing how to butcher them. If you have ever seen a child with dyslexia work with Legos, you can imagine what a caveman with dyslexia could do with an animal or a few rocks. The ingenuity is there, and it's instant.

Here's an example of that. When we first bought The Forman School, we couldn't afford decent fencing, and we had horses escaping. While the guys were gathering halters and bridles and feed buckets, I set out in the dark to find the horses with the Headmaster's daughter, who happened to have dyslexia. We found the horses grazing peacefully on a hillside. They were perfectly relaxed, but we knew that when the truck came over the hill, those horses were going to take off and be in the next county. And I said to the girl, "I'm not even wearing a belt, but if we could just have something to hang on to a couple of them then we'd be fine." Without missing a blink, she said, "Diana, we have our bras." In the dark, we took off our shirts, captured the horses, and had the two ringleaders firmly in tow by the time the guys drove up with the truck.

Seeing a solution in an instant by using a different way of thinking is a critical survival skill whether you are staring down a mammoth in front of your cave or staring down a skittish horse on a hillside.

Dyslexia Advocates,
What do you say?

Linda Selvin, Project Director, Consultant at Energy One

Whether or not dyslexia is a gift depends on the person you are talking to. A really frustrated ten-year-old may not recognize it as a gift at this point, but an incredibly successful adult whose success is linked to all the ideas that he bounces off the walls may see it differently.

Angel Hernandez
Frostig Center, Pasadena, California

I can show my emotions and who I am through art. People at Frostig buy my art, especially paintings and sketches. I am being impacted with new things every day. Teachers are willing to push me to succeed. The Academic Fair projects allow me to relate to others and share my views.

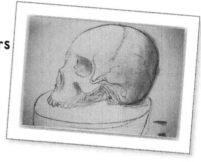

10
Anybody Up for Advocacy?

We have to advocate for children who have these differences so that they can have the opportunities and resources to achieve their potential - a potential which is not correlated with how well they read.
David Boies

Harvey,
What do you say?

Winston Churchill said it well in 1941: "Never give in, never give in, never, never, never, never – in nothing, great or small, large or petty – never give in, except to convictions of honor and good sense."

As parents, we have to advocate for our children, and teach them to advocate for themselves. We must be able to tell the teacher that this child is dyslexic, and we must teach our children to tell the teacher the same thing. Then we must make sure that the teacher understands what dyslexia is. Every teacher, every year. We must show the teacher our child's strengths, and insist on research-based remediation of our child's weaknesses.

I think of advocates as being a lot like Canadian Geese but without the honking. They fly in that V formation with a strong leader in the front, who sometimes gets tired and needs to back away—then another goose moves up to the front, ready for the challenge. My advocates changed throughout my life. My mom was my biggest advocate, but when she died, my guidance counselor, Steve Link, stepped up and took over the job. He had known my grandfather and my father, and it was one of the most fortunate days of my life when I realized that he would be there to connect with me, too. And there have been others when I needed them. I am grateful to all of them.

Many schools are doing an excellent job educating dyslexic children. But some schools are a little more difficult to work with, some even very difficult. Some schools won't admit that a child has a learning disability and will resist having a child tested. I was in a school district that put less energy into saving the learning disabled kids and more energy into getting rid of the troublemakers. One by one, they'd start pushing these kids out of the system. Problem solved. Changes in education law now compel districts to address problems that need to be fixed and try their best to save every one of their students. But the relationship between the district and your family can become antagonistic, and your child can suffer both educational and emotional damage.

I have met families that moved to other towns to find a district more willing to work with them. That's drastic. Some parents have sued their school district for tuition reimbursement, and sent their children to schools that specialize in teaching dyslexics. But that is also very expensive, emotionally draining, time consuming, and lately, parents rarely win. If that's your child falling through the cracks, never, never, never, never give in. And you knew that already.

We need a change in policy! Statistics show that the majority of inmates in federal prisons read at or below the third-grade level. Having an undereducated population is dangerous for our society – and expensive. So it just doesn't make sense. Each new president comes into office with plans for reforming education, but there is never enough time or money to make significant improvements. So the problems are passed on to the next president and to the next. Each president is looking for good grades while in office, but we have to look at a bigger picture.

We are all in this together as our country and our globe face huge problems. To come up with creative, currently unimagined solutions, we need to nurture every single kind of mind we've got. Policy change seems so right, but why does it also seem so slow?

Maybe it has taken this long, since Orton's word *strephosymbolia* first began to frighten bad spellers in 1925, because linear thinkers have had such a hard time understanding the concept of dyslexia and the value of cerebrodiversity. Our educational system is only just beginning to come around now, although there are isolated pockets of really effective schools with dynamic leaders that are models for the rest. There are some states and some countries that are beginning to see results.

We are right on the cusp of appreciation and respect for different types of learners. I think we will see a major change in our lifetime, but it demands the efforts of every one of us.

Alec Lang
The Kildonan School, Amenia, New York

At Kildonan they teach me so I can learn and it's a lot of fun. They set the homework to my ability. I am always full of ideas. I love to construct things - a chair in woodshop, a model car or an idea of how to improve the world.

Brain Specialists,
What do you say?

Gordon Sherman, PhD, Executive Director of Newgrange School and Education Center

Young children really need parents to advocate for them: to get the help they need, to change schools, whatever it takes. At the same time, parents must help children learn to advocate for themselves because at some point, as teenagers or as adults, they will have to fight for their learning differences (in a sense). They are going to need to teach people that they are not stupid, they are not disabled, but they learn differently, and can do some really wonderful things.

Mark Seidenberg, PhD, Senior Scientist, Haskins Laboratories

In the state of Wisconsin, the system does not recognize this identifiable condition. Denying its existence for whatever political reason is really unfortunate because it keeps kids who need resources from getting them.

There is variability in how hard it is for children to learn to read, but teaching methods assume that lots of support is coming from outside the school. The way that reading is taught now builds in a disparity between the haves and the have-nots, and we have a cascading, disastrous, rich-gets-richer kind of effect. We are going to see more and more low-literacy kids, and you have to wonder what will happen to them.

Gad Elbeheri, PhD, Executive Director, Centre for Child Evaluation & Teaching

You can't have a developed country where many of the people are illiterate. UNICEF and the United Nations recognize this, and have been working with countries over the past sixteen years to develop programs to address it. Countries have agreed on Millennium Development Goals to attain by 2015. One goal is to raise the standard of primary education. But you can't guarantee literacy for boys and girls alike if some have learning disabilities that nobody knows of. We realize that dyslexia has to do with basic reading, writing, and numeracy. And if we help those with dyslexia, we can help everybody as well.

Dyslexia is better known in the United States and the United Kingdom than in the Middle East. In Kuwait, a learning disability is a recognized form of a disability, and the government will actually provide funds for a learning disabled child to go to any school where we cater to individual needs. But the concept of dyslexia is not very well developed, although people are very supportive and understanding when we explain what it is.

When we say that individuals with dyslexia may have a combination of disabilities (such as having problems with reading and writing) and abilities (such as creativity), people say something like, "Oh, my uncle is like that. He is very brainy, but he doesn't like reading, and he won't write." They have a problem with the term dyslexia, and say, "Why can't we use an easier Arabic word instead of this funny word? It sounds like you have a problem with your back, disc pain or something like that." We tell them that this is an international term, and we need to use it. And then they are very receptive. And they are very keen on developing our awareness even more.

We have the typical situation of a teacher saying, "I appreciate that I have a dyslexic student in my class, but I also have twenty-four other children. How can I cater to the needs of my dyslexic child while at the same time not be unjust to the rest?" Or another question is, "How can I do the curriculum justice and reteach information at the same time?" All of these questions are there in the minds of our teachers, and there are also legal and other very challenging issues to deal with.

So we asked, *What have the U.S. and the U.K. been doing about this?* In the U.K., they have launched dyslexia-friendly schools by means of a whole-school approach where everyone is trained: all of the staff learns a basic-level reading program, is given information on dyslexia and taught how to use tools to identify children with dyslexia in the classroom. Even the nonteaching staff are trained in these areas. They work to increase the awareness of parents and offer training on how to help a child at home, so that parents can support the efforts of the school as cooperative partners.

We invited some experts from the U.K. and the U.S. to create some resources and models for early identification and to talk about teacher training. We have been working with two schools in Kuwait, trying to replicate programs from the U.S. and the U.K. to support these children in inclusionary settings.

The International Dyslexia Association is helping us disseminate sound scientific information about dyslexia, and they have come up with very simple, very accessible materials that parents can read to learn how to help their dyslexic children at school and at home.

So in the end, we have a project that was initiated in the U.K. and replicated in Kuwait with funding from our Ministry of Education and the United Nations Developing Program. It has been fascinating. Even the British experts who came and saw what we did congratulated us. It's a very good start.

Advocacy for dyslexia in the twenty-two countries of the Arab world is fairly recent but beginning to grow. In 2000, Kuwaitis established the Kuwait Dyslexia Association because of an aggrieved father who got no help for his son until he went abroad to acquire knowledge and take matters into his own hands. A similar situation happened in Egypt when a mother came to the United States for some help for her dyslexic daughter and went back to Egypt to establish the Egyptian Dyslexia Association. Work on the academic and advocacy level is also taking place in Bahrain, Saudi Arabia, and Jordan. Education on the whole, and special education and needs in particular, are critical issues in the Middle East; we are anxious to raise standards and awareness.

Guinevere Eden, PhD, Past President, International Dyslexia Association

The United States and England differ in how they handle the issue of dyslexia in terms of policy, research, and education. Parents in the U.S. are much more proactive. When I was a graduate student, I spent time in North Carolina and went to a local meeting of what was then the Orton Society, now the International Dyslexia Association (IDA). There were mums with nametags who were meeting and exchanging ideas, saying, "We need to do something for our children. We need to make sure researchers study this, and we need to make sure people in education help our children become better readers." That is something I had never seen in the U.K., and now you see even more awareness and policy changing. The other thing that's more advanced in the United States is the ability to do this kind of research. Doing fMRI is very expensive. At our institution, we pay $500 an hour to use the scanner. The money that is spent on research here is seven times more per person than it is in the U.K., so scientists here have more opportunities to get funding to support research. And research is necessary to better understand dyslexia.

Gordon Sherman, PhD, Executive Director of Newgrange School and Education Center

There is a lot of variability in terms of how states deal with dyslexia, and even whether or not they can use that term. I think the fact that some states do not acknowledge it, and do not provide structured language programs for children as they are learning to read comes from a lack of awareness and understanding of what dyslexia is. I believe that when people are educated about this, they will do the right thing.

We are losing generations of children who aren't able to read because they haven't been taught effectively. We have failed to understand dyslexia. We have failed to identify it. And many times, we have failed to put in place the most effective educational programs. That is a sad state of affairs. I know it is getting better, and I know all of us in this field are working toward making it better. But it is still going to be a generation or two before our schools are designed for people with dyslexia and before our society really understands the great value of those people who process information differently.

Dyslexics,
What do you say?

Billy Bob Thornton, Musician, Actor, and Filmmaker

My father was not the kind of guy who wanted me to go into anything artistic. It was either you're going to play sports, or you're going to get a real job. But it was obvious that I was not going to be a scholar of any type, so I focused on the one thing that I could do. I think many dyslexic people do go into the arts for this reason. But my mom always encouraged me and said, "Look, you're not stupid. You're really smart. The thing is, you just see things differently than other people."

Sarah Joy Brown, Emmy Award-winning actress

I knew I was never going to be an accountant, but I figured that once I learned how to work with my brain instead of against it, I'd be successful. I'd be okay. I hope to bring that message to other kids who might not have an advocate at home. I realize I can't help my daughter with her homework because it's already far beyond where I ever went in math, so I hired a tutor. But there are a lot of kids whose parents can't afford that. They may not realize that their inability to help their kids might keep their kids from realizing their full potential. Unfortunately, I've seen that happen.

Kendrick Meek, Former member of U.S. House of Representatives from Florida's 17th District

Before I got involved in the House bill to reduce class size, my daughter, Lauren, was in a kindergarten class with thirty-four children and one teacher. I started a movement in the state legislature to get smaller class size, but it didn't work. People run for office on this great idea, but then they don't work to make it happen.

I do have the ability to go to the school board, talk to the superintendent, and insist that I want this for my child. *Oh, she can get that. Your son, too. They will be placed in our smaller classes.* And the principal will be waiting at the door when I show up at the school of excellence. But what happens to everyone else? What about the kids whose dad isn't in the state legislature? If they don't have a parent advocate, they end up in a giant lecture hall classroom while tax cuts are going to the wealthy. We couldn't get our bill through the legislature, so we moved on a constitutional amendment in Florida to reduce class size. We got over eight thousand signatures, and finally it was approved by the Supreme Court.

I believe this will be one of the most substantial contributions that I could be a part of: to bring about a paradigm shift in the state of Florida and in the United States regarding our understanding of how many students can learn effectively in a class. Maybe if my classroom had been smaller, the teacher could have given a student like me a little more attention. If you put thirty-five kids in a classroom with one teacher, the teacher may have to make a terrible choice. Teachers want success, and they are being judged on success in high-stakes tests. They are taking the kids they can save, and the kids that they can't save are just going to sit there, and they might even end up a part of our criminal justice system if they don't come from a strong home and if they aren't strong themselves.

Reduction in class size is not the silver bullet, but it is a big part of the equation. We can't ask for success if we don't put forth an environment where children can learn and teachers can teach.

I have been working in Congress on putting more dollars towards dyslexia research. Teacher training is also very important. We have a better understanding now than we had when I was going to school, but there is still a lot of work that needs to be done. I think that the university system has to play a stronger role in building a curriculum for front-line educators and administrators who will be dealing with children with learning differences. It's like preventative maintenance. We must continue to research and learn. Special education teachers who were trained ten years ago are already dealing with a whole new ball game because of current research. We need a better understanding of the relationship between learning differences and high stakes testing. One size does not fit all. And let's not even mention the mountain of paperwork involved in the testing process.

Mckenna Carley

I came from a state where those who didn't pass the standardized tests found themselves stuck in third grade, or ninth grade, or tenth. Students found themselves graduating without a diploma, just receiving a certificate of completion. There are not a lot of colleges that want students with certificates of completion. They want kids with diplomas. They want kids who feel good about their educational experience.

The halls of Congress are filled with educators. But we need well-known people who have dyslexia themselves, such as the Hollywood crowd that is financially well off and has stepped up on other issues such as breast cancer or leukemia. We need these people to join us in the area of learning differences. Maybe some are still behind the curtain because they don't want to hurt themselves professionally or financially, but we need them to support increased research, understanding, and legislation. We need these people to come forth and be a part of change.

Sarah Joy Brown, Emmy Award-winning actress

My mom was an advocate for me in every way when I was a kid, but she was also dyslexic, so there were areas where she couldn't really help me. Maybe she didn't have the confidence to believe that she could. So I think I was my own advocate. Many years later, after I read the book, *The Gift of Dyslexia,* I gave it to her and said, "Here Mom –this is you, too." At first she just claimed, "I don't have a learning disability!" But then she read it and went on to graduate from college.

Kim Bucciantini, Graduate of The Forman School

My dad was my best advocate. He never gave up. When I was ten, things started to go downhill for me at school. He took it upon himself to help me, and he did a lot of searching for answers.

Kyle Morrissey, Graduate of The Kildonan School

My mother is my biggest advocate, without a doubt. My parents are fighting the public school system to get funding to send me to Kildonan. Without them, I wouldn't be here because we wouldn't have the money. Every year, my mom and dad get information together, and they go to the school board and fight for me. The best moment is when we get the funding. We go year by year.

Without Diana Hanbury King, I wouldn't be able to read. I can't even say in words how much she has helped me. Without her, I'd probably be illiterate.

Luke Bornheimer, Graduate of The Forman School

My mom is my biggest advocate. When I need funding for my tuition, and I have an IEP meeting where, basically, my town decides if I get to stay at Forman or be sent back to my public school, she is always right there. If she feels that it is better for me to do something, she's going to fight for it even if I am not in full agreement with her. I've got to give her credit for that and for not giving up when I'm flipping out on her. When I can't be positive about something, she is still able to really work hard and push through it. I guess that shows how much she really cares about me.

When I was evaluated and diagnosed, I still wanted to go back to my public school, and I felt that I could overcome these things. But my mom insisted, "You need *this* school. You need *this* support." I think that's the biggest thing a parent can do for a child – to do whatever it takes to get what the child needs.

David Boies, Attorney, *Time* magazine's 100 Most Influential People in the World in 2010

We live in a world today in which, far too often, people's self-respect is determined by how well they read and how well they do in school. We have tremendous pressure in our educational system to excel, and in many ways, that can be good. However, that pressure to excel forces many educational institutions, from grade school through college, to try to standardize people and to look at people as if there is only one measure of success. Often, that measure is how well and how readily they read.

Literacy is vital. Learning to read at some level is critically important, but how fast you read, how readily you read, and how many years it takes you to learn to read adequately are totally unimportant once you leave school.

People learn differently: with their ears, with their touch, and with their eyes (sometimes by reading, sometimes by observing). But frequently, at the most vulnerable stages of their lives, children are put into an environment in which the only thing that matters is how well they learn in a particular way, and I would suggest, a particularly artificial way. And because an artificial proxy is imposed on our children at their most vulnerable ages, it can lead many of them to give up, to act up, to quit school, and to be resentful.

It can lead school systems to figure out that the best thing to do is to give them less attention rather than more, to shunt them aside, not to teach them the additional skills they need to learn in different ways, but simply to try to teach them in the old way but at half strength. There is no reason that has to be. We know better. Our society as a whole knows better, but it is unwilling to commit the resources, the time, and the attention.

When my son, Christopher, graduated from Yale, he invited to the ceremony his childhood tutor who had worked with him for eight years and had made it really possible for him to achieve what he did. People who make those kinds of efforts contribute not only to the individual, but also to all of our society. It is unfortunate, but true, that the vast majority of children who have dyslexia today do not have that kind of opportunity.

That is why we have to advocate for children who have these differences so that they can have the opportunities and resources to achieve their potential, a potential that is not correlated with how well they read.

Parents,
What do you say?

Carol Hill, Parent and educational advocate for dyslexics

My husband and I have three children. We are dyslexic. For thirteen years, I have researched effective educational approaches, supportive home life, and emotional pitfalls of public schooling for students with dyslexia. For thirteen years, I have advocated for academic interventions. We "fought" our local public school district in the state of New York, working with Andrew Cuddy, an attorney who specializes in special education law. After several years with six different attorneys, we found that working with an attorney outside our geographic area and influence was a necessary component. I'm told that our son Callum's case accomplished the seemingly impossible: the hearing officer and New York State sided with him on all points. We received news of the decision in April 2009. These papers are online as part of public access.

I'm hoping that people will see this and realize, *Hey, there's a family with very few financial resources. It was just a regular mom who hung in there, used the Internet, and found out her children's rights. Her family stayed united, and the children are whole and happy.*

Warren Asplen

Most people do not know about our gag order, because we are not supposed to talk about that. We have four or five settlement agreements with the school — not made in the full-court press of an impartial hearing, but instead made when someone hears both sides of the story and makes a decision. And then someone in Albany decides if it was an accurate decision or not. This takes a long time, and it's very difficult and stressful.

All my research and professional debating never got me anywhere with our district. I thought if I could learn more and express it better, I would get the officials to understand me — wasn't so. I even brought in expert people, but officials did not want to hear them and did not implement what they recommended. I found out later that the district has to consider other options, but it doesn't have to implement them.

All of these decisions are in public records at the SRO website at www. sro.nysed.gov. If you look for *Decisions*, you will see them from 1990 through the present. They run about thirty pages each. They never state the name of the child or the school district, so a similar lawsuit could be going on within your district, and you would never know it. It is all confidential, and the downside is that makes it difficult for parents to join together because we don't know who the other parents are. Representing years of struggle within families, the cases where parents appealed the Impartial Hearing Officer's decision are lengthy and complex. Most cases end in the words of the State Review Officer: *Appeal is dismissed*. But some end in: *Appeal is withdrawn*.

Our settlements are not about winning. They represent an agreement between two parties, and they involve give and take on both sides. But my children have received no apology from the district, and that bothers me a tremendous amount.

What will it take to change things in our schools? It seems like a simple shift to incorporate models that work, but it is so very difficult to influence changes at the grassroots level. I believe that change has to come at the policy level with changes in state or federal laws. I would feel ecstatic if my children wouldn't have to work this hard when their own children with genetically linked dyslexia need a particular type of instruction in school.

Diana Naples, New York branch of International Dyslexia Association

You think educators know what they're doing. Well, I realized they didn't, so that's why I decided to get involved. I found that if you really want to talk to your principal, just get there at six thirty in the morning. I would plan to take the day off and just sit there until they could see me. I'm sure I've been very annoying, and I don't like being like this. I would much rather be in the back seat and be more helpful, but sometimes you have to be forceful. I've tried to bring to the school certain programs I've found through the IDA, and this has fallen on deaf ears. When I bring in people to talk to parents, there are sometimes just a handful of parents there, although the school has more than a thousand students.

Carole Bellew, Parent of Luke Bornheimer

The tragedy is that many kids who have a learning disability can't speak for themselves. Unless they have a parent who advocates, or a teacher who has enough energy to advocate for them, they can fall to the wayside. Yet, some of these kids are the brightest and the best, with such potential to grow.

Carol Hill, Parent and educational advocate for dyslexics

Many times, I have seen the surprise, disillusionment, and anger in parents who come to realize that their public school is not being straightforward with them, and is not looking after the best interests of their child. They had no idea that they were on different sides! It eventually dawns on parents intuitively that if they leave their child in an unhealthy situation much longer without intervening, they will be cooperating in a type of educational and emotional neglect. It is a harsh realization that public school officials see a child's educational need as a threat to policy, to personnel, to professional development budgets, to administrative versus citizen control, to the status quo of testing and identifying students at risk, to the distribution of government money, and to perceived real estate values versus percentages of district students with learning challenges.

Diana Naples, New York branch of International Dyslexia Association

I try to point people in the right direction at monthly workshops. We try to educate parents so they are more informed and therefore, more empowered. We invite parents to come and hang out with other parents going through the same issues and find out what they did. I know I found it worthwhile talking to the parent of an older child when my child was younger. Now I feel like I'm one of the senior parents, and I want to try to help any other child that's out there.

Carol Hill, Parent and educational advocate for dyslexics

I know that moving a bureaucracy through a mass of red tape is slow, and complicated, and very difficult. But if one mom from upstate New York can go this far, then certainly our elected leaders can work to change policy to ensure that there will be appropriate and effective classrooms for all our children.

Teachers,

What do you say?

Margie Gillis, EdD, Senior Scientist, Haskins Laboratories

Parents want to help their children, but in order to do that effectively, they must educate themselves. They have to learn everything they can, and they have to figure out who is going to affect change. If they happen to have connections, they have to use those connections. I believe they must take the energy that they put into their own children and say, *I have to do this for all kids,* because there are so many kids out there with no advocates and no parents fighting for them. We must call them to arms and say, *As the parent of a child who has struggled, you know what this feels like. You know in your gut how horrible this is. You don't want other*

*kids to go through this, so you must take your knowledge now, figure out
how you can help other parents to be aware, and lead those parents.*

I really believe parents are the key to changing policy. If parents get
angry enough and organize in a positive way that empowers them
to believe they can bring about change, I think that would send the
message to our policy makers, our legislators, and our leaders that
we are not going to stand for this anymore. We have too many kids in
pain who are going to struggle their whole lives because they didn't
learn to read in first grade.

Robin Winternitz, Dyslexia advocate and educational consultant

Education is just not what it should be or what it was designed to be.
All kids have a desire to learn. It is an innate feeling; it should be there.
Schools today squelch that, and that shouldn't happen. Advocacy is
something that can help turn that around.

Margie Gillis, EdD, Senior Scientist, Haskins Laboratories

I have gotten very involved in going up to the State Department of
Education, learning who the players are, who the policy makers are,
and finding legislators who are going to move this agenda, so that we
don't continue to perpetuate this problem.

We have a huge achievement gap in Connecticut, and I believe the reason
is that we haven't taken ownership of the problem. We have to take this
to the national level, but a lot of people are not willing to challenge the
status quo. It isn't easy to do that. You are not popular, and you really
make a lot of people mad. But that is what it takes to change something.

In Connecticut, we have 169 school districts, and that means we have
169 boards of education made up of lay people who may be selecting

a reading program. How do they go about doing that? Unfortunately, money talks. Major publishing companies with gobs of money court the powers that be, whether it is the superintendents, the curriculum directors, or the board members, to sell them their program. So unfortunately, a lot of money is spent on garbage, on materials that do not have substantive research behind them. Because of No Child Left Behind and Reading First, districts have to buy materials that are considered to be reading research based. Well, it's easy to say, "Yeah, we have these components. They're all included here," but all reading programs are not created equal.

Here is what I want to say to legislators: "Do you know how big a problem this is? Are you aware of the percentages of kids who are not reading on grade level in fourth grade? Do you know that 88 percent of our African-American students are reading below grade level? Eighty-five percent of our Hispanic students? Fifty-nine percent of our Caucasian students? This isn't just kids who live in poverty, this is across the board. This is *all kids* struggling. For what? Why? Because we are not doing what works, and we know what works. We have thirty years of research coming out of places like Haskins Laboratories. People have dedicated their research lives to exploring the most effective ways for teaching reading. Why isn't it happening? How can you sleep at night knowing this?"

It costs about $23,000 a year to keep a person in prison. It costs about $11,000 a year to educate a child, so if you care about the economics of this, that's a no-brainer. If I had a chance to talk with people in Washington who could get this whole effort moving, who really understand reading issues at a deep level, and could make things happen, I would fill their ears.

If I could, I would make sure that every child has access to education, and the earlier, the better. And it would be fun. It would be playing with language, talking, building those language skills that are so critically important to being a literate adult. Language, literacy, and books can open up worlds, but you can't access them if you can't read. So I would make sure that all children have access to an educational system that affords them that important human right of learning to read. And then I would develop it from there. Once a child reaches proficiency, the sky is the limit.

Daniel Ashby
Triad Academy, Winston-Salem, North Carolina

After one year of private school, I was asked to leave because I couldn't keep up with the other students. The school didn't know how to handle my learning challenges. At Triad, my teachers believe that I am intelligent and capable of learning. They also have the knowledge to be able to teach kids like me to read. I am a visual artist,

and my designs have won awards and were featured in the Brian Ayers Memorial Art Exhibit, an international exhibit celebrating the unique talents of students with learning disabilities.

Dyslexia Advocates,

What do you say?

Linda Selvin, Project Director, Consultant at Energy One

I advise parents to find workshops or monthly groups, to gain every piece of information they can on dyslexia, from what their children with dyslexia experience to ways to advocate for their children. Being around other parents, they learn the social and emotional issues that accompany dyslexia. They find out what it's like to oppose the decisions of a school and argue a case.

To be able to advocate for their children, parents need a specific diagnosis of the educational problem. They also need an understanding of the laws of their city and state, along with an understanding of the politics at their local school. In addition, they need to know how the school operates and which people to approach to obtain the most effective services for their child. Otherwise, it's not going to happen. Parents need to be able to go back in six months and ask, "Is this program actually working for my child?" It's not enough to start the program and let it go for a year. Parents have to go back and see the progress, to find out whether the tutor or teacher is providing the proper instruction and following it up. It comes down to parents needing to educate themselves about their child's needs and about the system.

There is wonderful advocacy training out there. We recommend the books and parent programs of Peter Wright, an advocate, a lawyer, and also a dyslexic. In his presentations across the country, he stresses documentation and follow-up, and knows the process very well.

I recently read an article written by Jo Anne Simon, a lawyer for people with disabilities. I think she really hit the nail on the head regarding accommodations for people with dyslexia. She quoted a parent whose child, a slow processor, was not allowed extra time on an exam, and compared the situation to a child with a hearing loss who is denied the use of a hearing aid and a nearsighted child who is not allowed to wear glasses during an exam. I hope this analogy makes the need for accommodations clearer for those people who are so concerned that we are giving an undeserved advantage to some children.

I'd like to tell a policy maker that any type of learning difference can be addressed at a very early age. When I'm talking to politicians, I know what their priorities are. They set their budgets, and they set their priorities. They are concerned about money, and I tell them, "You're going to save a lot of money if you address learning issues and effective teaching for those issues at an early age. Deal with it now, and don't wait until later when the condition is worse and the treatment costs more."

Isaiah Stockdale

Politicians need to understand what learning disabilities are and how they can be remediated. They need to understand that it's not brain surgery, it's a technique. And they can save lots of money, educate many more children, and create a much more dynamic work force with early intervention. It is to their benefit. And it benefits all of us.

Peggy McCardle, PhD, National Institute for Child Health and Human Development (NICHD)

I'm the acting chief of the Child Development and Behavior branch at the National Institute of Child Health and Human Development (NICHD). That's one of the institutes at the National Institutes of Health in Bethesda, Maryland. Our branch funds a lot of research on foundational information about reading, including how children learn to read, what goes wrong when they don't learn to read, and how to either prevent that or intervene.

There is federal funding for reading and reading disability research, and some of it is labeled dyslexia research. The Child Development and Behavior branch funds all aspects of child development including: social, emotional, general biological, cognitive, and language. And our institute has a major commitment to that research, but we also have large portfolios and networks in reading research, including issues involving adolescent literacy, adult literacy, bilingual literacy, preschool learning, and school readiness. The federal investment is not only at NICHD; there are other institutes at the NIH that fund reading or dyslexia-related research: the Neurology Institute, the National Institute of Mental Health when there is a relation to psychopathology, the National Institute of Deafness and Communications Disorders, and the Institute of Education Sciences (the new research institute in the U.S. Department of Education that funds a substantial amount of work on reading and reading disabilities).

Before all of the research was centralized at IES, the Office of Vocational and Adult Education and the Office of Special Education and Rehabilitation Services within the Department of Education had partnered, and they still have ongoing commitments for support for several of our literacy networks. The National Institute for Literacy also contributes research dollars to the literacy network.

This substantial and well-coordinated investment in reading, reading disability, and dyslexia research has been going on for some time and will continue. I'm very happy to say that it's had broad bipartisan support because the politics of reading are that everybody wants to see kids succeed. Everybody wants kids to be able to learn. And regardless of whether we have a Democratic or a Republican administration, there is a major commitment to looking at evidence-based practices to achieve this goal.

Whether we like how No Child Left Behind is being implemented or not, and regardless of the issues we have with testing kids, we do need to know on a broad base how kids are doing. The Reading Excellence Act of 1998 was the one that started this whole terminology of evidence-based instruction and scientifically based research, and since then, it has continued and will continue, and I think that is a good thing. We need to do a better job for America's children.

Elaina Saracino

Ultimately, research will influence policy, but we like to see policy based on convergent evidence, not on fads, not on philosophies, but on replicated studies that are done with high quality methods. Therefore, policy makers can have confidence in embracing new findings and calling for their implementation, and teachers can have confidence that new findings are worth changing their practices.

It is costing us a huge amount not to educate people. It is a tragedy any time a child is not given opportunities to live up to his potential. No matter what the job, from entry level to jobs that require a specialized degree, success is unlikely without literacy. Estimates vary, but roughly half of the people in our criminal justice system cannot read. Fortunately, there are some efforts out there providing intensive interventions, and a lot of them have been effective, but we need to hit this at prevention and intervention levels. We've got to be more effective from preschool through college. We see college students and graduate students who are still not optimal in reading and writing, especially at higher levels.

It is very important to continuously instruct, intervene, and improve, but while we wait for those preschoolers with whom we are doing a great job to come through the pipeline, there is still a bump of teenagers stuck in the pipe, building a clog. We can't afford to lose teenagers. We can't afford to lose anybody. And the cost is not only at school district levels, or community levels, or state levels, it's at the global level. When you look at how we're stacking up against other nations, we're not on top. We're not going to do better economically unless we do a better job educationally, especially with reading and writing. Our legislators and our business people need to pay attention to this so that we can compete in a global economy.

We need to implement good solid reading instruction and intervention for every child. *Amen.* Sorry, I get wound up.

Samantha Miller
Holy Spirit School, Great Falls, Montana

My teachers here are very understanding. Most of the time, they respect my request not to call on me to read during class. When they are picking someone, I hide behind the person in front of me, and try not to make eye contact. I have learned to use my strengths to overcome my weaknesses. And I have a passion for writing poetry and designing clothes.

11
Any Advice for Parents?

I think parents should make sure their kids who can't learn in a traditional way never feel that they are less than anyone else.
Joe Pantoliano

Harvey,
What do you say?

Parents, stop worrying. I know you're up against all kinds of things. Dyslexia sounds terrible. *Dyslexia.* But your child is not disabled because someone has given him a label. If you can understand his language, then he is communicating. He might not spell too well. He might read slowly. So what? Give him extra time to read. As long as he learns to read, nobody is going to time him with a stopwatch out here in the real world.

Learn as much about dyslexia as you possibly can. The more knowledge you have, the less panic you will feel. Try to embrace it, and find your child's gift. What is he really good at? Does he love music? Building things? Animals?

If your child is really having a difficult time learning to read, find teachers, tutors, or schools that use multisensory methods. Meanwhile, find other ways to keep the information coming in. If you had a blind child who was trying to learn to read, you would never yell at him and say that he could see better if he worked harder at it. You would teach him to use Braille, and let him access books that way. So if your dyslexic child likes Harry Potter, read it to him, or get him audio books. There are many books available for any age and area of interest, written at a lower reading level. I do think it's really important to get your kid to be able to crack the code, but there are a lot other ways to pass around information. Talking to each other and telling stories worked well for our ancestors.

I did eventually learn to read, not at school, but with one-on-one tutors outside of my public school system. Few families can afford to send a child to a school for children with learning disabilities for $50,000 a year. And not every family can afford to pay a one-on-one tutor. But home schooling might be an option. If you can home school your child, look for dyslexic home schooling courses, and invite other dyslexic children to join you. A number of schools for children with dyslexia began this way. It's like solving a puzzle to figure out your child's education. But that's okay. You may be a bit of an outside-the-box thinker, yourself, if you know what I mean.

Brain Specialists,

What do you say?

Carolyn Cowen, Executive Director, Carroll School Center for Innovative Education

When parents receive a diagnosis of dyslexia for their child, it is really easy for them to lose sight that accompanying the dyslexia are gifts and strengths. I would counsel parents to become informed, to learn as much as they can about the field, and to find out what their rights are. There is a whole laundry list of things that parents need to attend to, and usually they have a pretty steep learning curve. But along the way, I would counsel them to pay attention to the child who is going through this experience. It is important that they do their best to translate what's going on for the child and always, always, in that process, convey a message of support and appreciation for what makes their child unique.

Gordon Sherman, PhD, Executive Director of Newgrange School and Education Center

Identify early; intervene early.

Ken Pugh, PhD, President and Director of Research, Haskins Laboratories

What I would first tell parents is that there's evidence that the brain of a child with learning disabilities is tremendously plastic, and by plastic, we mean capable of reorganizing itself. We've seen in a number of studies in the last five years that when we give intensive learning opportunities over an extended period of time, there is a shift in brain response. Even kids who are not necessarily going to become Derek Jeter can learn to hit a baseball. The environment, if enriched, will have profound effects on the brain.

Gordon Sherman, PhD, Executive Director of Newgrange School and Education Center

If I were giving advice to parents, I'd be really militant: *Advocate for your child.* Don't take any nonsense from anyone in the school system. If indeed there is a problem, make sure your kid is identified, and that she is remediated immediately. And that's tomorrow. You can't wait and hope things get better. You can't listen to people who say, "Let's wait six months or a year, and it'll probably clear up." That's wasted, wasted time.

You need to start immediately with your child, making sure she doesn't feel disabled because the environment isn't structured properly for teaching her. You need to get her into a program of multisensory, structured language, working on phonemic awareness and phonological processing. There are many kinds of programs like that, and they may differ a little bit, but they all have the key to teaching people with dyslexia how to read. The earlier you implement that, the better.

As a parent, you can't take any baloney from anybody about your kid. She can be damaged, her self-esteem can plummet, and she can develop psychological issues, so you need to support her and make sure she's getting what she needs.

Stay away from the quacks out there. There are a lot of alternative methods that just waste time. Make sure you are in an effective program, and that's the remediation side, but that is only half of what you need to do. Just as immediately, you want to work to keep up the self-esteem of your child, and help your child understand what this is – that it is not a global issue that affects everything. If your child is labeled with a disability, it is hard for her to understand that she still has talents. Identify what your child's strengths are, and do whatever is necessary to give her experiences that really develop those strengths. It might be that your child is a good athlete, or musically talented, or an actor, or really good in math but processes math differently. Whatever it is, focus on that as much as you do the remediation.

Pop Quiz #8

Often the key for a dyslexic learner is meeting a teacher who seems to understand what it is like to be dyslexic and who can explain the theory behind the difficulties that he/she experiences. This is one reason that it is important for teachers to learn the advances in:

    a.   inutrition, theology, and music.

    b.   psycholinguistics, neuropsychology, and behavior genetics.

    c.   traditional reading and writing methodologies.

    d.   none of the above.

(Answer at the back of the book)

Dyslexics,

What do you say?

Aaron McLane, Special Effects Artist

Parents should never, never doubt their children when they are asking for help. Yes, children do like to bend the truth, but when they tell you something isn't right, you must believe them with every ounce of your heart, because that is something a kid wouldn't normally tell you. If they tell you they have trouble paying attention, you don't say, "Well, you just need to work harder at it." No, there is probably something about it. It may not be something that you have thought of, or that you had to deal with, but there is probably something.

Kim Bucciantini, Graduate of The Forman School

No matter how hard your kids are struggling, don't give up because there are options out there that you just have to search for. I knew that I was struggling, but if I had the right opportunity, I would succeed. My dad eventually found Forman for me. You have to keep searching, and eventually you will find the right place. It is worth it when you see your kids' grades go from D's and F's to A's and B's.

Keaghan Hamilton, Graduate of The Forman School

Parents should be straightforward with their kid and not just say, "Oh, you're fine." They shouldn't sugarcoat that the kid has dyslexia, because there is nothing to sugarcoat. There's nothing wrong with having a learning difference. It's something to be excited about because it is a challenge. I know some parents don't want to admit that their kid has a learning difference, but they should find out all they can about it, learn to live with it, and get the help the kid needs.

Lauren Retallick

The kid's reaction is probably going to be like mine was: *Wow, I'm stupid. I'm not going to get anywhere, and everyone is going to see me as different.* I'd always tell my mom, "I don't want to do this anymore – I hate having dyslexia." But I know now that you should get the kids tested and get them the accommodations they need, because later in life, they're going to see that's what really helped them. They may not like it at first, but later on, they'll look back on it and say, "Wow, if my parents hadn't done this for me, I would never have gotten as far as I have." As much as I complained to my mom about having to be tested, I'm really grateful that she made it happen.

Billy Bob Thornton, Musician, Actor, and Filmmaker

Two of my kids have dyslexia, two out of the three. I grew up with a father who was not an encouraging person, and I think you can either be like the parent you had, or you can be the polar opposite. That's what I've done with my kids, never been anything but encouraging. I'm the kind of doting father they have to push away: "Come on, Dad, my buddy's over there. Don't hug me, I'm sixteen."

Joe Pantoliano, Emmy Award-winning actor

I think parents should make sure their kids who can't learn in a traditional way never feel that they are less than anyone else. During my life, feeling like I was less almost destroyed me because I turned to drugs and alcohol to fill up that hole.

Any Advice for Parents?

Eric Steinberg, Parent and dyslexic

Don't settle. Don't allow the system to ignore your child's needs because these are often incredibly intelligent children, and they can learn so much. You must be your child's advocate, and you must make sure that the system does not shame your child. I've had to work for twenty-five years to recover my self-esteem, and I cannot emphasize enough the importance of that piece.

Zach Capriotti, Inmate at State Correctional Institution

The advice that I have for parents is to give children as much support as possible – mental support. The most hurtful word is *retard*. If you do not support your children mentally, study with them, and help them, they'll break. They'll have low self-esteem and feel bad about themselves, and then they may act out in the wrong ways. And they may end up in jail like I did.

Charlie Phillips, Artist

Parents should get their kids tested, see what works best for them, and never give up. They shouldn't think they did something wrong. Their kids are just wired a little differently, and everyone else is too, in some way.

Stephen J. Cannell, Writer, Producer

One thing you have to do is make sure your child does not give up on himself. That's the big danger with this condition. When he is getting a lot of bad grades, he's being put in special education classes, his perception of himself starts to go down. Your job is to combat that. Your job is to say this is a gift. Your child may have ideas that are much more interesting than the kids who are getting straight A's.

I had football to help me, but you can look for whatever it is that your child is good at, whether it is theater, or art, or video games. It doesn't matter. Make a big deal of those successes because the one thing you want to preserve is your child's self-worth. Once he gets out of school, this problem kind of goes away, you know.

David Boies, Attorney, *Time* magazine's 100 Most Influential People in the World in 2010

Parents, you are there to help, not increase the burden and make the child feel even worse about what's happening. You've got to find a way to be encouraging, to be positive, to focus on the things that can be done, and to advocate for your child.

My worst moments were watching two of my children struggle with dyslexia, watching how hard it was for them, watching them doubt themselves. It has been harder for me to be a parent of dyslexics than to be dyslexic myself.

Now, I would tell parents to be patient and not get discouraged. Try to take a broader view, a longer view, and see that dyslexia does not threaten your child. It is going to affect a part of his life, and he is never going to be free of it, but once he gets out of school, it becomes much easier. He can read less, and he can learn more. He can choose an occupation where he can work creatively and not rely on his reading. It's probably a bad idea for a person with dyslexia to become a proofreader, but there are lots of other professions out there.

Parents,
What do you say?

Carol Hill, Parent and educational advocate for dyslexics

Because of our years of experience as parents researching dyslexia and challenging the school district, other parents frequently come to us seeking answers. The concerns they have are basic: *What is dyslexia? Why can't my child speak clearly at this age? My child seems too hyper and can't hear me when I give multiple directions. She cries when she does her homework, and I don't know how to help her. His teacher says he's just immature, but I think it's something more. I had the same problems in school myself. This one child of ours isn't like his brothers or sisters, and we work twice as hard with him. She can understand everything when I explain it to her, but she can't read her textbooks. Is there something I can do to help her at home? Can Sylvan help? Will he ever be able to read? What do I tell her when she is crying and frustrated with her homework? Which of these outside tutors know what to do? We've tried several already with no luck. Where do I go for this outside independent testing I am reading about in my rights? Will the ADD medicine help with dyslexia as well? How do I cope with this feeling of anxiety and sadness? I just want what's best for him. Please, tell me what you know so I can help my child!*

Parents would find us at local meetings, at the farmers' market, in the grocery store checkout line, at our bus stop, at musical performances, at the post office, at local advocacy meetings, and through awkward phone calls that they felt embarrassed about but forced themselves to make for their child. We have become a stop on a sort of underground railroad because people in our community find it so difficult to get answers through official channels.

In our culture, there is outdated ignorance about dyslexia and prejudice against anyone who cannot read, write, and spell well. With speech delays from slower language processing speeds, our family's language challenges were even more public and confronted even more cultural taboos. When we were seemingly walking toward hell, not many people wanted to follow us. But now that they see our children growing, laughing, adapting well, and expressing their intelligence and creativity, people come to us wanting to read our compass. They are more willing to travel this difficult road when they see it leads in the direction they want to go. They are grateful and relieved to learn from us and to benefit from the many shortcuts that our experience has taught us on that same journey.

I invite people who are seeking me out for answers to come to my house for a pot of tea. They often stay five, six, seven hours, and don't want to leave. I let them know that because of a legal agreement, I can't tell them about my son's situation specifically, but I can share with them all I have learned about dyslexia. I can tell them where they can learn more so they can move forward, and relax, and have some joy return to their lives. There are knowledgeable professionals who write and speak and petition for policy change. There are successful programs out there, there are advances in technology that can make a huge difference. And there are tremendous and varied strengths in their child that are key to productive and prosperous jobs in his future.

When parents come to me, I use expressions they think are taboo. They come knowing that dyslexia is something people make fun of, and they fear that the label of dyslexia is going to ruin their child. They fear that dyslexia will prevent their child from having a full life. They're afraid of the whole concept, but when I give them a little information about where to get answers, they start to relax and even laugh a little bit.

First, I advise them to compile a binder like the one our attorney had us compile, which allows any professional the opportunity to absorb and understand the child's history. I tell them to keep accurate paperwork because this is not about opinions, but actual evidence and examples of how the child is doing. Second, I recommend reliable, thorough, independent testing to supply parents with the scientific basis they need to advocate for their child. The testing also provides an individual profile of the child, so parents can improve their own understanding of weaknesses. And finally, I state honestly that all the research, professionalism, documentation, meeting attendance, and blood, sweat, and tears I shed never made a significant change in any one of my children's educational programs. Legal representation opened doors that had been firmly closed. Even now, with legal representation, dealing with our district to secure and keep successful programs is an ongoing trauma for our family, but it remains the only way to offer our children full, productive lives. So we persevere.

There's an Internet site called Wrightslaw, a good place to start to learn the ins and outs of what you need to know, because you are definitely swimming upstream. When you are fighting bureaucracy, you need to know your stuff.

Cary Spier, Parent of Sarah Spier, dyslexic, and documentary filmmaker

Angelica Goovdhue

My advice for any parent with a dyslexic child is to stick with her. Don't give up on her. Don't treat her like you think there's something wrong with her. Embrace it. Fight for this kid. Every child needs a person in her life who believes in her and says, "I am one hundred percent behind you. I'm going to be here when you get home, and I'm going to be here when you get up, and I'm going to wipe the tears off your face. I'm going to keep putting you out there, and if the school is not right and if the teacher is not right, we'll find a new school and a new teacher. You're going to be fine. You don't need to be like everybody else." Fight for your child because if you don't, she'll fall through the cracks. Nobody else is going to do it for you, so you have to fight for her every single day.

Voncille Wright, Parent of Jo'Von Wright

Listen to your child. I regret not listening to Jo'Von when she would tell me that she didn't understand or it was hard. Even when she wasn't talking, I didn't listen to her mannerisms. I didn't listen to how she would become a shrinking violet when she was around other children her age who could read while she couldn't. I just didn't listen to her.

Close out all the negative energy around you because people will always give you advice. I had to learn to close my ears to everything that people were telling me. One person actually said to me, "Beat that child! She's just trying to drive you crazy. Just whip her, and she'll come around."

Never give up. Make sure that you maintain faith in your child. There's a scripture that we say at church, *Faith is the substance of things hoped for and the evidence of things not seen.* Sometimes we didn't see Jo'Von's progress, but we never gave up hope, and I hope we instilled that in her: never give up.

Teachers,

What do you say?

Nancy Cushen White, EdD, Associate Clinical Professor and Learning Disabilities Specialist

I would never tell a parent to wait and see what is going to happen with a struggling child. Even if it is a moderate learning disability, the sooner appropriate teaching occurs, the sooner the student starts to feel confident and can move on. If you can't read, and if you can't write, it just takes all the joy out of what should be wonderful and joyful.

Dana Blackhurst, Headmaster, Camperdown Academy

Parents say, "Here's my son. He can't write. He's dyslexic. He can't spell." Okay. Think about what would happen if your son now is twenty-five years old, and goes up to his boss and says, "I can't do that because I'm dyslexic." Boss says, "I don't care what you are, just get it done. I don't care how you do it, just get it done." That's what we should be instilling in the kids in first, second, third grade. Parents, back off, this kid can do it. It's the will to try that's more important than anything.

Micah Sitzman
Holy Spirit School, Great Falls, Montana

I put great effort into my work. One of my greatest strengths is remembering   details. I can use my ability to see things in pictures and go back to them in my mind to see details that some other people wouldn't even notice.

Dyslexia Advocates,
What do you say?

Linda Selvin, Project Director, Consultant at Energy One

A teacher is certainly very aware of every student in the class, but over and over again, it is the parent who actually notices, *There might be a problem here, and we need to look into this.* The teacher may say, "It's okay. Let's give this child some more time, maybe another six months or a year." I would say to that parent, "No, look into it now. Keep your own eyes open, get a professional to look at this child, and get a diagnosis."

The school must provide an evaluation for a child if a parent requests it. Parents who are not satisfied with the evaluation can arrange for a private evaluation, but the school may not agree with it or even recognize it. Parents may need to find an advocate or a lawyer to help them seek reimbursement. The process can be costly. My office has an information referral specialist and a list of advocates and lawyers who work with parents of children with disabilities. In New York City, the public legal organizations are familiar with learning problems and how to get necessary services.

12
Any Advice for Dyslexics?

Discover who you are and take your solo, baby.
Malcolm Alexander

Harvey,
What do you say?

Kids, you are in great company! There are thirty-five million Americans who have dyslexia. Dyslexics are found all over the world, wherever there is a writing system. Einstein may have had dyslexia, so if neurotypical people find out you are dyslexic, tell them that your nonlinear processing is more like Einstein's than their pale, linear, dots-connected-by-a-ruler version. I think it's sad that schools are not set up for nonlinear thinkers. Maybe linear thinking students could be taught to solve problems more as we do, with ingenuity and, um, magic.

Also kids, tough times may be ahead; but no matter how difficult school gets, you can get through it. Do not give up. There are certain pitfalls that you will have to watch out for, so try to find someone to help you who values cerebrodiversity.

Focus on what you really love to do and what you're really good at — and work on getting better and better at that (because that is what you're going to get paid for once you leave school behind). You're probably not going get paid to do those things you're really bad at, and no one is going to care anymore that you can't do them. You'll have to figure out ways to use compensating mechanisms to help you get over a few rough spots like writing checks. But remember, you are able to think outside the box, and you have a lot of ingenuity.

Brain Specialists,

What do you say?

Ken Pugh, PhD, President and Director of Research, Haskins Laboratories

I would remind kids that they are normal, beautiful people, full of infinite potential, who have a wealth of endless, untapped talent that needs to be honored. I would remind families that we should never confuse a difficulty in learning to process language and read with a limitation on what kids can accomplish in life. There are so many great examples of folks who struggled with this who went on to make magnificent contributions to the world around them.

If kids who struggle with reading and language begin to stand up for themselves and take no prisoners, this can be nothing but good for cognitive and emotional development.

Gordon Sherman, PhD, Executive Director of Newgrange School and Education Center

The first thing we say to someone who has just been diagnosed is that your brain is fine. It processes information differently. There is nothing abnormal about it. It is wired differently, and this can be a good thing if you use those wiring differences to your advantage. This can be a good thing if you are in a school setting that understands and can design instruction for those differences.

Dyslexics,

What do you say?

Annette Jenner, PhD, Assistant Professor, Syracuse University

Be proud of who you are and what you've accomplished. At The Forman School, we hear that our brains just work differently than everybody else's. I've dedicated my life to figuring out how my brain and the rest of the dyslexic brains out there work. I haven't figured it out yet, but I can tell you this: I'm glad I have the brain I have, and that it works the way it does. Yes, it's hard to read and write sometimes, and most of the time that can get a little annoying, but it has made me who I am, and it has allowed me to view the world in a unique way. And it's this uniqueness that makes the world a great place.

Olivia Hanson, Graduate of The Forman School

Don't be scared. Don't let anybody else put you down. Be like me. And you'll be shocked if you see me ten years from now because I'll be better than ever. Just keep that high feeling about yourself.

Charlie Phillips, Artist

Don't give up. Try to find out what works well for you. It might not be what your teacher wants, and it might take you a few more steps, but it's not wrong. Just don't give up.

Sarah Spier, Founder and President of Mwambao Alliance, Mwambao Primary School, Tanzania

You've just got to trust life. Run with what you're good at, and what's meant to happen will happen. It will all fall into place eventually. It's okay that you can't read fast. In the scheme of life, it doesn't matter.

Sarah Joy Brown, Emmy Award-winning actress

Bradley Morell

I prefer to focus on dyslexics who have been successful, rather than on kids in juvenile hall who don't know how to read. I wouldn't want the kids we are trying to encourage to think, *Well, that's where I'm gonna end up. That's where kids who can't read go.* I think it's a better idea to look at positive role models, people like Tom Cruise or Muhammad Ali. It's important to show kids that people who learn differently may struggle in school, but they also have gifts. So many of our children have gifts to give the world, and if that gift isn't spelling, that's okay.

Open your eyes if you see a learning difference in yourself. Realize that there's so much good to be found there. Welcome to the club. Don't be embarrassed. I work on that every day. Just embrace it. It's who we are.

Keaghan Hamilton, Graduate of The Forman School

Have fun with it. Find what you're good at, and prove people wrong.

Phil Marandola, Graduate of The Forman School

Don't give up. Keep on plugging away at it, and eventually, you'll get it. Just work and work and work and work, and just keep on working. That is why dyslexics make it because they have that work ethic. They keep going, and they don't give up. They persevere. Things come easier to the kids who don't have dyslexia, and they don't have to work or don't choose to work. They don't develop that work ethic. They don't care.

Sarah Spier, Founder and President of Mwambao Alliance, Mwambao Primary School, Tanzania

If you don't get it, you don't get it! Go onto something you understand! I'm never going to get algebra. I'm never going to do anything that has to do with algebra. And you know what? Life goes on. It's okay not to understand everything and not be perfect at everything.

Malcolm Alexander, Sculptor

After I realized I was dyslexic, I didn't want any more Malcolm Alexanders to have to experience what I did. So that's when I wrote the Exeter letter. It's been in books, it's been all over. In it I explain those early years, the pain, the humiliation. Now I go out and tell young people to do what I did. I had to find the substance, that gift within me that no one else has. Mine alone. That is what gets me up on that podium. I tell them that as an artist, I have built lots of monuments. I work with clay and mud. I tell them if I can build something with mud, there are tools within *you*, and *you* can build your monument, too. When I look out over audiences, I've often said,

"Hey, if I can help one of you find your gift, it's worth getting up here and making an ass of myself."

Cary Spier, Parent of Sarah Spier, dyslexic, and documentary filmmaker

Life is a great equalizer once you get out of school. All of a sudden, it doesn't matter if you are dyslexic. Nobody knows, and nobody cares. Of course, the reason nobody knows is because we are so good at hiding it.

Billy Bob Thornton, Musician, Actor, and Filmmaker

When I was a kid, I wasn't aware that what I had was dyslexia. Now kids know, and that's good. I would tell them, *Embrace it.* I think that having dyslexia is kind of cool, like having a battle scar that nobody else has.

I pushed through all this stuff and made it somewhere in my life where I might not have gotten without dyslexia. You've got to take what you get and make it a strength. When things are harder for you, you come out stronger. I may have three fingers, but watch me throw this curveball.

Annette Jenner, PhD, Assistant Professor, Syracuse University

It is one thing to joke about being dyslexic with other dyslexics on the way back from a soccer game, but it's a totally different thing to go up to your first college professor and talk to her about it. However, introducing yourself right away provides you with several advantages. First, it will ensure that your name will be the first that your professor will learn. In addition, it will allow your professors to know ahead of time that you may need extra help. It's always better to ask before you're in trouble. This is not an easy thing to do, but just remember this: the class is filled with students who have graduated from high school and earned good enough grades and SAT scores to be accepted in college, just as you have. But you are much smarter and have worked much harder to get there. You have overcome some significant difficulties to get there. In all my years of being a student, and there have been quite a few, I've only run into one professor who didn't want to take the time to understand my learning needs.

Luke Bornheimer, Graduate of The Forman School

It can be real tough to find out you have dyslexia, especially at the end of middle school, going into high school. You feel so connected to the peers you've known for nine or ten years, and now you may have to change schools. I would tell kids to make the sacrifice with friends, and understand that in the end, it is going to work out better.

I think it is not necessarily the book lessons that teachers give to kids that are the most valuable. A lot of people can just teach exactly what's in the book, but a good teacher is the one who gives the kids life lessons. A good teacher can motivate kids to really succeed at whatever they want to do in life.

Malcolm Alexander, Sculptor

Kids with dyslexia have an advantage. They know what failure is, and when you know what that feels like, what more can you lose? I tell them, "Get out there. You may fail again, but you know about failure, and you will find your way." Too many other people quit when they meet their first defeat. But we don't quit because we don't have anything else. I became one hell of an athlete with my anger. I know all of us dyslexics are angry. Harness that anger, and you can conquer the world. Don't harness that anger, and it will defeat you.

Olivia Card

When the dad is a successful banker and the son can't add, don't destroy the young kid. He might be the next Rembrandt. That's been the story of my life. I think it's kind of like the phoenix rising up from the ashes. I'd crash and burn. So what? Get up again. Over and over again. You get stronger and stronger and stronger.

And that all goes back to what I've been saying about dyslexia – you are different. Discover who you are, and take your solo, baby.

Contributors

Malcolm Alexander Art Center College of Design, Pasadena CA. Sculptor. Notable artworks include sculptures of Joe DiMaggio and Johnny Bench, Jimmy Stewart, and 18-foot monument in Valdez, Alaska that pays homage to those who built the Alaskan pipeline. Frequently speaks at dyslexia seminars and conferences about his own experiences with dyslexia.

Carole Bellew Parent of Luke Bornheimer.

Dana Blackhurst BA, Erskine College. Headmaster, Camperdown Academy, Greenville, SC; board member, Andre Agassi Preparatory School, Clark County Public Education Foundation. Recognized for his work by the Orton Dyslexia Society, P. Buckley Moss Children's Charities, the State of South Carolina, and the South Carolina Independent School Association.

Billy Blanks Fitness guru, martial artist, actor, and inventor of the Tae Bo exercise program.

David Boies BS, Northwestern University. Magna cum laude, Yale University School of Law. LLM, New York University. Attorney, included in *Time* magazine's 100 Most Influential People in the World in 2010. Represented Vice President Al Gore during the 2000 election recount, and named runner up for *Time's* Person of the Year. Served as special trial counsel on behalf of the US Department of Justice in a suit against Microsoft for antitrust practices.

Luke Bornheimer Graduated from The Forman School; member, National Honor Society.

Sarah Joy Brown Played Carly Corinthos and Claudia Zacchara on the daytime drama General Hospital from 1996 to 2001; earned three daytime Emmy Awards. Also appeared on *Without a Trace* and *Crossing Jordan*.

Kim Bucciantini Graduated from The Forman School; earned academic honors.

Stephen J. Cannell BS, University of Oregon. Writer/producer whose credits include *The Rockford Files, Baretta, The A-Team, Wiseguy, The Commish, 21 Jump Street*, and *Profit*, considered a forerunner of the cable-style dark drama. Died, 2010.

Zach Capriotti Inmate at the State Correctional Institution at Albion, PA.

Daniel Cortez Graduated from The Kildonan School; received Janet Mayer Alumni Award and Academic Effort Award. Currently attending University at Redlands, Redlands, CA.

Julie Costanzo MA, MFA, University of California, Berkeley, MS, State University of New York at Albany; SDA, State University of New York, Cortland; BFA, University of Michigan, Ann Arbor. Former director of curriculum and instruction, Otsego Northern Catskill BOCES; special education teacher, Oneonta High School, Oneonta, NY. Co-editor, *Dislecksia: The Book* (2012).

Carolyn Cowen EdM, Harvard Graduate School of Education; executive director, the Carroll School Center for Innovative Education; coordinator, Dyslexia Genotyping/Phenotyping Initiative; president, Communication by Design; cofounder, Learning Disabilities Network; recipient of the Alice H. Garside Award from the New England branch of the International Dyslexia Association. Among numerous publications, coauthored "Dyslexia with 20/20 Vision: Where Will We Be in Ten Years?" IDA Perspectives on Language and Literacy Winter 2010.

Nancy Cushen White EdD, University of San Francisco; MEd, College of Notre Dame; BA, University of North Carolina. Associate clinical professor and learning disabilities specialist, Division of Adolescent Medicine, University of California San Francisco School of Medicine. Consultant for SpEd-SFUSD, working with special education teachers to develop and refine multisensory structured language curriculum and instructional strategies in their classrooms.

Guinevere Eden PhD, Oxford University, BS, University College, London. Past President, International Dyslexia Association; director, Center for the Study of Learning; associate professor, Department of Pediatrics, Georgetown University Medical Center. Among numerous publications, coauthored "Grey Matter Volume Changes Following Reading Intervention in Dyslexic Children." Neuroimage October 2010.

Gad Elbeheri PhD, University of Durham, UK; BA, Alexandria University. Executive director, Centre for Child Evaluation & Teaching, which combines research and practice on specific learning disabilities across the Arab world; project manager, Early Learning Challenges & Disability Project, United Nations Development Programme, Kuwait; board member, International Dyslexia Association. Among numerous publications, co-authored "Assessing Children with Specific Learning Difficulties: A Teacher's Practical Guide" (2011).

Steve Frost PhD, University of Connecticut; MA, University of Connecticut; BA, College of the Holy Cross. Senior scientist at Haskins Laboratories. Among numerous publications, coauthored "Phonology Constrains the Mental Orthographic Representation." Reading and Writing 14.

Eric Gardner MFA, USC School of Cinema/Television in Los Angeles; BA, Columbia University in New York City. Has worked on independent feature films and nonfiction television for over 20 years as a writer, director, producer, and editor. Received multiple Emmy nominations for his work as an editor on the CBS series, *Survivor.* As a director, won best film at the Big Bear Lake Film Festival for *Under the Influence.* Co-wrote and produced *Breakaway,* and was senior editor of *Alien Autopsy: Fact or Fiction,* one of Fox's highest rated specials. Credits also include producer of *Queenas* and co-producer of *Great Streets: Champs-Élysées* for PBS. Co-Executive produced *Love in the Wild* for NBC. Editor and producer of *Dislecksia: The Movie* (2012). Currently, he is Co-Executive Producer of *Shahs of Sunset,* a docusoap series for Ryan Seacrest Productions and Bravo. Member of The Academy of Television Arts & Sciences and The Directors Guild of America.

Jeffrey Gilger PhD, University of California, Santa Barbara; MA, University of California, Santa Barbara; MS, California State University, Hayward; BA, California State University, Hayward. Associate dean for discovery and faculty development, Purdue University College of Education. Scientific advisory board member for the Dyslexia Foundation. Among numerous publications, coauthored "Brain Morphological and Neuropsychological Profiles of a Family Displaying Superior Nonverbal Intelligence and Dyslexia." Cortex 42.

Margie Gillis EdD, University of Louisville; BA, Connecticut College. President of LiteracyHow, Inc.; Senior scientist at Haskins Laboratories; former director of Haskins Literacy Initiative; worked as Haskins mentor in Stamford at the International School at Rogers Magnet; president, Connecticut branch of the International Dyslexia Association; co-founder of Smart Kids with Learning Disabilities. Publications include "12 Ways to Help Preschoolers Develop Literacy Skills," *Smart Kids with Learning Disabilities.* Web.

Tomi Guttorm PhD, University of Jyväskylä, Finland. Among numerous publications, co-authored "Newborn Event-Related Potentials Predict Poorer Pre-Reading Skills in Children at Risk for Dyslexia." Learning Disabilities 43.

Keaghan Hamilton Graduated from The Forman School; earned academic honors; received the Athletic Award, and Forman's highest award, the Headmaster's Award.

Olivia Hanson Graduated from The Forman School; received the Julie Ripley Forman Award for top female student; member, National Honor Society.

Marcia Henry PhD, Stanford University. Past president of the International Dyslexia Association; former director of the Center for Educational Research on Dyslexia at San Jose State University. 2000 recipient of International Dyslexia Association's Margaret Byrd Rawson Lifetime Achievement Award. Speaks frequently at conferences, and writes for and serves on the editorial boards of several professional journals; provides professional development seminars on teaching reading and language arts and consults with several school districts and states on informed reading instruction.

Carol Hill Educational advocate for dyslexic children for over 13 years. http://dyslexiathetrencheswithsuccess.com/About.html

Jack Horner Regents' professor of paleontology at Montana State University; curator of paleontology at the Museum of the Rockies; recipient of a MacArthur "genius" award; consultant and model for the lead character in *Jurassic Park* films. Publications include *How to Build a Dinosaur: Extinction Doesn't Have to Be Forever* (2009).

Harvey Hubbell V Documentary filmmaker and dyslexia advocate; wrote and directed multi-award-winning documentaries, including *Electronic Road Film* and *Loop Dreams*. Producer and director of *Dislecksia: The Movie* (2012).

Annette Jenner PhD, Harvard University. Assistant professor, Department of Communication Science and Disorders at Syracuse University. Recipient of an RO3 award from the National Institutes of Health entitled "Neurobiology of Spelling in Skilled and Disabled Readers."

Diana Hanbury King MA, George Washington University; BA, Honors, University of London. Fellow of the Academy of Orton-Gillingham Practitioners and Educators; served on the faculty at Sidwell Friends School and the Potomac School; founder of the Kildonan School, and Dunnebeck Camp for dyslexic students. 1990 recipient of the Samuel Orton Torrey Award. Publications include *English Isn't Crazy!: The Elements of Our Language and How to Teach Them* (2000). Currently writes, lectures, trains teachers, and tutors students in reading.

Che Kan Leong PhD, DLitt, University of Saskatchewan; MA, BA, University of Hong Kong. Research professor emeritus, University of Saskatchewan; recipient of International Dyslexia Association's Samuel Torrey Orton Award, and Margaret Byrd Rawson Lifetime Achievement Award. Former editor-in-chief, *Annals of Dyslexia*. Among numerous publications, coauthored *Literacy Acquisition: The Role of Phonology, Orthography and Morphology* (2003).

Steve Link BA, Western Connecticut State University; MA in Adolescent Psychological Counseling, Southern Connecticut State College. Attended Yale University Department of Psychiatry's Drug Institute. Former editor of the *CPGA* (*Connecticut Personnel and Guidance Journal*). Retired after 30 years of counseling adolescents; continues to work *pro bono* in educational and legal cases for disadvantaged, exceptional, and addictive/dependent youths.

Phil Marandola Graduated from The Forman School.

Peggy McCardle PhD, MPH, BA. Chief of Child Development and Behavior Branch, Eunice Kennedy Shriver National Institute for Child Health and Human Development (NICHD) of the National Institutes of Health; liaison for the NICHD with the National Institute for Literacy;

NICHD liaison to the National Reading Panel. Lead editor of *The Voice of Evidence in Reading Research* (2004).

Aaron McLane Special effects artist; Production Assistant, *Kamen Rider*.

Kendrick Meek BA, Florida A&M University. Former member of U.S. House of Representatives from Florida's 17th District, 2003–2011. Launched an amendment to reduce class size that was approved by voters but not by the required 60 percent.

Einar Mencl PhD, Dartmouth College; BA, University of Maine. Senior scientist, director of neuroimaging research, Haskins Laboratories. Among numerous publications, coauthored "Phonological Awareness Predicts Activation Patterns for Print and Speech." Annals of Dyslexia 59.

Kyle Morrissey Graduated from The Kildonan School.

Diana Naples Information and Referral Specialist, New York branch of International Dyslexia Association.

Richard Olson PhD, MA, University of Oregon, BA, Macalester College. Professor, Department of Psychology, University of Colorado; faculty fellow, Institute for Behavioral Genetics; director, Colorado Learning Disabilities Research Center, past president, Society for Scientific Study of Reading. Among numerous publications, coauthored "Gender Ratios for Reading Difficulties." Dyslexia 3.

Phyllis C. Orlowski MA, State University of New York at Albany; BS, University of Connecticut, Storrs; BS, State University of New York at Oneonta. Multisensory (TPRS) Spanish teacher at Oneonta High School, Oneonta, NY. Dyslexia advocate. Coeditor, *Dislecksia: The Book* (2012).

Joe Pantoliano Studied at HB Studio, New York City. Actor; film credits include *Risky Business, The Matrix, Memento,* and *The Fugitive*.

Awarded Emmy for Outstanding Supporting Actor in *The Sopranos*. Founded charity organization *No Kidding, Me Too!* to foster education and awareness of mental illness.

Charlie Phillips Artist.

Joyce Pickering SLP/CCC, CALT/QI, HumD. Executive director emeritus of Shelton School and Evaluation Center; director of the Perceptual Development Center and the EC Program, Natchez, MS; director, Reading Study Foundation; dean, EC Program and Primary School, Sao Paulo, Brazil; cofounder, Brazilian Dyslexia Foundation. Publications include *Montessorians Helping Students with LD in Sensorial Curriculum* (2010).

Colin Poole BA, Connecticut College. Painter and sculptor. Exhibitions include Bucks County Gallery of Fine Art, Appleton Museum of Art, Museum of Texas Tech University. Corporate clients include U.S. Postal Service, National Geographic Society, PBS.

Ken Pugh PhD, MA, Ohio State University; BS, New York Institute of Technology. President and director of research at the Haskins Laboratories; member of the faculty at the Yale University School of Medicine. Among numerous publications, coauthored "Early and Late Talkers: School-Age Language, Literacy and Neurolinguistic Differences." Brain 133.

Sylvia O. Richardson MD, MA. Distinguished professor of communication sciences and disorders and clinical professor of pediatrics at the University of South Florida. Past president, Orton Dyslexia Society; certified speech/language pathologist and certified Montessori teacher as well as a physician. Publications include "Historical Perspectives on Dyslexia." Journal of Learning Disabilities 1.

Dee Rosenberg MA, Montclair University. Director of education at Newgrange School and Education Center; certified learning disabilities teacher consultant; educational diagnostician; president of New Jersey branch of International Dyslexia Association.

Philip Rubin PhD, MA, University of Connecticut; BA, Brandeis University. 2010 recipient of American Psychological Association Meritorious Research Service Commendation; chair of the National Academies Board on Behavioral, Cognitive, and Sensory Sciences; member of the NRC Committee on Developing Metrics for Department of Homeland Security Science and Technology Research; senior scientist and CEO at Haskins Laboratories; adjunct professor, Department of Surgery, Yale University School of Medicine. Among numerous publications, co-authored "Speech: Dances of the Vocal Tract." Odyssey Magazine Jan 2007.

Evelyn Russo PhD, MA. Mentor, Haskins Laboratories Literacy Initiative; Publications include "Does Your School Reading Program Make the Grade?" *Smart Kids with LD*. Web.

Roger Saunders MS, BS, Southern Methodist University. Clinical psychologist who contributed to early diagnosis and remediation of dyslexia. Past president, International Dyslexia Association. Helped found Jemicy School for dyslexic children in Owings Mills, Maryland; Odyssey School in Baltimore, MD; Rawson-Saunders School in Austin, TX. Helped organize the Dyslexia Tutoring Program in Baltimore, a free service to low-income children and adults. Died 2006.

Mark Seidenberg PhD, Columbia University. Professor of psychology, investigator, Communication and Cognitive Processes Unit of the Waisman Center, University of Wisconsin; senior scientist, Haskins Laboratories. Publications include "What Causes Dyslexia?" Trends in Cognitive Sciences 15.2.

Linda Selvin BS, Wagner College. Project director, consultant at Energy One; past executive director of Agenda for Children Tomorrow; past executive director of the New York branch of the

International Dyslexia Association; past director of programs at Learning Leaders.

Gordon Sherman PhD, University of Connecticut. Executive director of Newgrange School and Education Center; former director of Dyslexia Research Laboratory at Beth Israel Deaconess Medical Center; former faculty member at Harvard Medical School. Past president of International Dyslexia Association; recipient of Samuel T. Orton Award, Norman Geschwind Memorial Lecture Award. Publications include "Dr. Gordon Sherman on Brain Research and Reading." *Schwablearning. org*. Web.

Delos Smith Completed a degree in political science and economics; served 46 years on the Conference Board; reported regularly on global financial markets and management on CNBC, CNN, and BBC; senior economist for the Security Executive Council; economics professor, Fordham University; national board member and financial advisor, International Dyslexia Association.

Arlene Sonday MA, University of St. Thomas; BA, Gustavus Adolphus College. Founding fellow and first president of the Academy of Orton-Gillingham Practitioners and Educators; 2009 recipient of International Dyslexia Association's Margaret B. Rawson Lifetime Achievement Award. Publications include *Sonday System—Let's Play Learn (RTI Curriculum)* (2009).

Cary Spier Parent of Sarah Spier. Documentary filmmaker, writer/director/producer. Worked as in-house producer for one of the largest production companies in Hollywood. Real estate agent, Santa Fe Properties.

Sarah Spier Founder and President of Mwambao Alliance, Mwambao Primary School, Tanzania.

Eric Steinberg Dyslexic parent of a child with dyslexia.

Joan Stoner EdD, MA, University of Nebraska. Fellow of the Orton-Gillingham Academy, president of the Nebraska branch of the International Dyslexia Association; educational consultant, Stoner Consulting and Tutorial Services. Publications include Orton Emeritus Series: *College: How Students with Dyslexia Can Maximize the Experience, 2nd Ed.*

Billy Bob Thornton Musician, actor, and filmmaker; wrote, directed, and starred in the Academy Award-winning film, *Sling Blade*. Other films include *Armageddon, Primary Colors, Pushing Tin, The Man Who Wasn't There, Bad Santa, and Eagle Eye*.

Ovid Tzeng PhD, Pennsylvania State University. Professor, National Yang-Ming University; fellow, Academia Sinica. Publications include *Neurolinguistics: A Chinese Perspective* (1996).

Wendy Welshans Environmental science teacher, The Forman School; biologist; director of the Rainforest Project.

Tom West Author. Presents to scientific, medical, art, design, computer, and business groups in the U.S. and overseas on highly talented dyslexics, visual thinkers, and the rise of computer graphics technologies. Publications include *In the Mind's Eye* (1991, 1997, 2009, with new Introduction by Oliver Sacks, MD) and *Thinking Like Einstein* (2004).

Robin Winternitz Dyslexia advocate and educational consultant; member, Citizen Advisory Committees for Harford County Public Schools; member, Learning Disabilities Association of Maryland.

Voncille Wright Parent of Jo'Von Wright.

... and a final thanks

I would like to extend a personal thank you to all who have worked on this project to raise awareness about dyslexia.

I thank all of the students who provided school and life experiences to share in this book. You are our dyslexia diplomats. Thank you to your parents, families, schools, and teachers.

Academy in Manayunk: Simon Shankweiler

Churchill Center and School: Christopher Faust, Genevieve Greer, Eliza Milton

Eagle Hill School: Tess Crocker

The Friendship School: Emily Bruder, Jacob Garwood, Naomi Adrianne Royster

Frostig Center: Jonathan Marhaba, Angel Hernandez

The Gow School: Gabriel Suarez, Walker Meers, Brendan Buckley, Desi Gialanella

Hamlin Robinson School: Sarah Berneker

The Hillside School: McKenzie Renee Telatovich, Meg Bennett, Jorge Miranda

Holy Spirit School: Micah Sitzman, Samantha Miller

Hudson Valley Community College: Elisha Wenzel

The Kildonan School: Ky Nicyper-Meryman, Mara Felman, Alec Lang, Marken Aboitiz

Morning Star School: Stephanie Elgendi

Riverside School: Dennis Miller, Kayla Rider, Stewart Mancano

Spring Valley School: Devin DiPiazza

The Shelton School: Katie Kirkland

The Springer School: Malakai Graham

The Siena School: Shayan Afshar

Triad Academy: Damali Archie, Daniel Ashby, David Lord

I am grateful to all of the student artists from the **Newgrange School** in Hamilton, New Jersey, and **Greater Plains Elementary School** in Oneonta, New York. Your drawings of what it feels like to "get it" and "not get it" in class come straight from your hearts and add so much to our book. I send my thanks to Desi Gialanella, Forrest Valiquette, Noah Schlitt, Maria Farrell, Warren Aspen, Robbie Tonner, Catherine Lusius, Nicky Harold, Domonic Cooper, Nancy Xun Mi, Melissa Richter, Jessie Warzybuk, Olivia Card, Chyanne Wellman, Elaina Saracino, Isaiah Stockdale, Alyssa Bredin, Scott Zangara, Austen Marshall, Andrea Shaw, Bradley Morell, and McKenna Carley.

And finally, thanks to all of the **Captured Time Productions** interns, advocate moms and dads, volunteers, helpers, including Jodie Siwik, Richard Collins, PhD, from Brehm Prep, Jack Parry, Bill and Jeanne Quain, Rio Gaiser, Max Gialanella, and many, many, more who gave time, energy, and passion to this book and to our mission.

Harvey Hubbell V

Harvey Hubbell V's Biography

Growing up, I was the apple of my mom's eye. I had a spring in my step and not a care in the world. Then I went to school. In 1966, when I was six years old in first grade at Hawley Elementary School in Newtown, Connecticut, I remember my teachers having a private meeting about me. "He can barely write his first name," said Mrs. B. "I noticed he doesn't know how to hold his pencil," said Mrs. W. They didn't know I was listening, or maybe they did and didn't care. But I did hear them.

That was only the beginning of when I started to feel a little inadequate to my fellow classmates. On my report card, one teacher noted, "You'll find Harvey an alert, cooperative, interesting, bright, happy child who contributes much orally to the class. He does exceptionally well on a one to one basis but is completely lost in group instruction." My mother knew I was smart, but most teachers did not see that, and my mother worried a lot.

My parents had me tested to find out what was wrong. In second grade, they found out I was dyslexic. Little was known back then about what to do with a dyslexic. Testing continued on me year after year. Testing never ends when you are dyslexic. I learned to read outside of the school system through a series of one-on-one tutors. In 1977, I graduated from Newtown High School. My class rank was 275 out of 325 students. Perhaps I should add that I just barely graduated. Of course, the teachers had passed me along to get rid of me, but I had few skills to survive in the real world.

During one of my attempts to go to college, it was confirmed that I was not college material. My English professor excused me from class permanently when he learned that correct spelling and grammar didn't exist in my writing. My ideas were not judged, but my lack of structure in writing was. "Those skills should have been learned prior to entering college classes! You may be excused now, Mr. Hubbell," he grumped.

Years later, it became apparent to me that I was born at the wrong time to get help with dyslexia in school. It wasn't until 1975, a few years before I graduated from high school, that the first laws were passed to identify students with learning disabilities and to support their rights to education. It was too late for me. At sixteen years old, I was already considered damaged goods. I felt that my teachers and others did not understand me. If I had been born later, maybe I would not have had to go through all of the pain and struggles that I experienced in school. Instead, I would close my eyes and daydream. I'd bury my face in my arms on the desk and invent movies.

Being a visual thinker, I gravitated toward the film industry. For years I worked on any TV show, feature film or commercial that would have me. Sometimes I worked for just food, shelter, and even clothing. Eventually, through hard work and determination, I started telling my own stories through movies. It turned out that people liked them, and I won some awards. So I made more films and won even more awards – 9 of which were Emmys.

My documentaries have won more than 50 film and video festival awards. I wrote and directed the multi-award winning comic documentary, *Electronic Road Film*, which received an Emmy for Outstanding Entertainment Program. *Loop Dreams,* my first feature-length documentary, won the Gold World Medal for Comedy at The New York Festivals and three Emmys for Outstanding Entertainment Program, Individual Achievement for Directing, and Program Writing.

To support my documentary habit, I sometimes work on feature films, including a turn as Columbia Pictures' community liaison for *Mr. Deeds,* shot on location in New Milford, Connecticut. In 2003, the Senate Majority Leader appointed me to the Connecticut Commission on Culture and Tourism. I served as co-chair of the CCT Film Committee, and was instrumental in getting the CT film tax credit laws enacted.

My latest project is a documentary on dyslexia titled, *Dislecksia: The Movie,* slated for release in 2012. I wanted to make this film to show how much things have changed since I was going through school. Sadly, not much has changed and too many kids are still falling through the cracks much like I did. I hope this film will become the conversation starter needed for change to occur with regards to public policy and public awareness, early intervention and teaching training, and create the opportunity for hope for dyslexics and their families.

Acknowledgements

This whole adventure began when close friend and advisor of Harvey Hubbell V and Eric Gardner, Walter Fiederowicz, urged them to find a use for all the footage that didn't make it into the movie. He quickly helped them realize how a book could be one more tool for parents and advocates to be able to have. Eric and Harvey soon saw how useful it would be for advocates to be able to give a book to teachers, superintendents, or policymakers. By presenting the educators with the latest scientific data and helping them to notice if a student might be dyslexic, this book could be another 'voice' to advocate for them.

We had years of interviews and information in video footage from filming, but we could only fit 85-minutes of that into the actual film. The Captured Time Production interns spent hours upon hours, logging verbatim all the words said in the dozens of interviews that took place.

Enter our Co-Editors: Julie Costanzo and Phyllis C. Orlowski. They began to compile these interviews in a way that would answer questions about dyslexia in a fun, informative way. When these two teachers weren't working on their own curriculums and lesson plans, they spent their days and nights piecing together this book.

That manuscript was then handed over to "Harvey's Frontal Lobe" and the "Grammar Nerd" of Captured Time, Aimee Santos and Rio Gaiser. These two put blood (from the paper cuts), sweat (the office was pretty hot some days), and many curse words into proofreading and editing this book. There were arguments across the room about whether or not to use a semicolon or a dash. There were late night work texts with one asking the other if they really found certain interviews relevant to the book or not. There might have even been a tussle or two over comma placement. Thankfully, the two had enlisted help from a friend in Florida to catch their mistakes and work as a tie-breaker of sorts. She put in extra time and effort to help us make sure this book got done and was done right. The editorial savior even sent over the latest edition of *The Chicago Manual of Style*, making Rio giddy with delight and causing Aimee to roll her eyes at her co-workers' nerdiness. Luckily, intern Catherine Greene, helped sort out any other editorial battles between the two.

During this time, there were many others that popped in to offer words of advice, their talent, and much needed encouragement about how completing this book would benefit so many. Among these people are Paul Cohen, Holly Shapiro, Christopher Blake, Sheila Moses, Bill and Jeanne Quain, Jack Parry, Eugene Orlowski, and our very own Eric Gardner.

We would also like to acknowledge our friends that found time to read our proofs of the book and review it for us in the midst of their busy lives. To name a few: Andrew Kavulich, Dr. Hugh Catts, Beth Ravelli, Dr. Nancy Mather, and Dr. Lydia Soifer. And we could never forget about the interns now (along with the ones to come in the future) that have to lug around boxes of this book to any event we attend. We will not, however, acknowledge any back problems they may have in the future.

Finally, we give credit to where credit is due to all past Captured Time Production interns, advocate mom and dads, volunteers, helpers, including Jodie Siwik, Richard Collins, PhD, from Brehm Prep, and many, many more who gave time, energy, and passion to this book and to our mission.

How To Contact Us

Interested in learning more about *Dislecksia: The Movie* or *Dislecksia: The Book, Companion to the Documentary Film*? There's a multitude of ways to gain information about our projects, from joining our mailing list to Liking us on Facebook. Please see below for how you can keep up to date with **Dislecksia: The Movement**.

If you would like to bring Harvey to your area and host a screening *Dislecksia: The Movie* at your school or organization, contact us to discuss the possibility of fundraisers, panel discussions, community events, and the like. The sky is the limit with these events, and we are pleased to work with you to structure a win-win situation for all involved.

Furthermore, if your company is interested in becoming a corporate sponsor, please reach out so that we may send you our corporate sponsorship package. Sponsoring an evergreen film project such as this would be a great way to get your company's name out there to the same educational markets we reach out to. We share the same mission of teaching kids how to read, so let us help get the word out about your company. We'll be traveling around the United States and the world for years to come promoting, so why not come along for the ride with us?

During the course of editing (and re-editing) *Dislecksia: The Book, Companion to the Documentary Film*, Harvey Hubbell V started The Hubbell Difference Foundation with the purpose to blend the worlds of philanthropy, filmmaking, academics, farming, and community action. It has received 501(c)(3) status as a public foundation and can receive tax-deductible donations. For more information on the foundation and its projects, please visit *www. thehubbelldifferencefoundation.com*.

Finally, if you are interested in volunteering for **Dislecksia: The Movement**, please be in contact to see how you can help, whether it's with a film festival in your area or making phone calls on our behalf. We couldn't have gotten this far without our advocates on the ground, but we have a long way to go and we need each and every one of you!

How to Contact Harvey and the Dislecksia: The Movement crew:

Phone/Fax: 860-567-0675
Email: *captimepro@gmail.com*
Mailing Address: 51 Hutchinson Parkway
Litchfield, CT 06759

Film website: *www.dislecksiathemovie.com*

Company website: *www.capturedtimeproductions.com*

Like us on Facebook: *www.facebook.com/dislecksiathemovie*

Follow us on Twitter: *www.twitter.com/dislecksiamovie*

Join our monthly Newsletter mailing list: *http://eepurl.com/krjsv*

P.S. Did you love the book or the movie? Send us your comments for inclusion on the *Dislecksia: The Movie* website!
We would love to hear from you!

Bring Dislecksia: The Movie To A Town Near You!

Interested in hosting a pre-release screening of *Dislecksia: The Movie*?

We look forward to partnering with you to organize successful *Dislecksia: The Movie* events around the world!

Contact the Producers of the film at 860-567-0675 or via email at **_captimepro@gmail.com_** to learn how to bring Harvey, his crew, and *Dislecksia: The Movie* to your town.

We will work with you to meet your needs.

Whether your objective is to spread awareness about learning differences, promote your school or organization, fund raising, teacher training, or other.

We have had incredibly successful events.

Our screenings range in size from blockbuster standing room only crowds of 500 to intimate groups of 20, across all types of venues.

We are happy to assist you in organizing event-related activities.

Promote and make the most of your event by including panel discussions, TV appearances, radio and newspaper interviews, *Dislecksia: The Book, Companion to the Documentary Film* book signings, meetings with student groups, parent organizations, community leaders...and more.

We look forward to hearing from you and hope to be in your town soon. Thank you!

Answers to Pop Quizzes:

Pop Quiz #1
Answer: b acquired
Source: Moats, Louisa. "Teaching Reading Is Rocket Science: What Expert Teachers of Reading Should Know and Be Able To Do." AFT Teachers, Mar. 2004. Web.

Pop Quiz #2
Answer: c   80%, 90%
Source: Foorman, Barbara, Jack Fletcher, and David Francis. "A Scientific Approach to Reading Instruction." LD OnLine. CARS, 1997. Web. :

Pop Quiz #3
Answer: c   almost never
Source: Juel, 1988; Francis et al., 1996; Shaywitz et al., 1999, "Waiting Rarely Works: Late Bloomers Usually Just Wilt."

Pop Quiz #4
Answer: b   2nd, 3rd
Source: "Preventing Reading Difficulties in Young Children." The National Academies Press. Ed. Catherine E. Snow, M. Susan Burns, and Peg Griffin. 1998. Web.

Pop Quiz #5
Answer: b 75%
Source: Lyon, G. Reid. "What Principals Need to Know About Reading." National Association of Elementary School Principals (NAESP), Nov.-Dec. 2003. Web.

Pop Quiz #6
Answer: c 2-10%
Source: Walsh, Kate, Glaser, Deborah, and Dunne Wilcox, Danielle. "What Education Schools Aren't Teaching about Reading and What Elementary Teachers Aren't Learning." Reading Rockets, 2006. Web.

Pop Quiz #7
Answer: a   identified early, if they have a supportive family and friends and a strong self-image, and are involved in a proper remediation program.
Source: Kraft, Sy. "What Is Dyslexia? What Causes Dyslexia?" www.medicalnewstoday. com. Medical News Today, 27 Apr. 2010. Web.

Pop Quiz # 8
Answer: b psycholinguistics, neuropsychology and behavior genetics.
Source: Rack, John. "The Theory and Practice of Effective Teaching for Dyslexic Learners." 2005. Web.

18695463R00147

Made in the USA
Charleston, SC
16 April 2013